DISCARD

IT'S
IN
THE
BIBLE!

IT'S IN THE BIBLE!

A Practical Historical and Sociopolitical Perspective of Scripture

ARTHUR PADILLA

Library of Congress Control Number: 2019912775
ISBN: Hardcover   978-1-7960-5612-9
                   Softcover   978-1-7960-5611-2
                   eBook   978-1-7960-5610-5

Scripture quotations marked KJV are from the Holy Bible, King James Version (Authorized Version). First published in 1611. Quoted from the KJV Classic Reference Bible, Copyright © 1983 by The Zondervan Corporation.

Print information available on the last page.

Rev. date: 08/31/2019

To order additional copies of this book, contact:
Xlibris
1-888-795-4274
www.Xlibris.com
Orders@Xlibris.com
800190

CONTENTS

CHAPTER 6   JEHOVAH IS AN INSTIGATOR OF EVIL

INTRODUCTION

We have been lied to about the god of the Bible about what he is and what he stands for.

In this book, I will take a practical, unbiased approach in describing the significant historical, social, and political influence biblical scripture has had and is having on human society today with an emphasis on the USA.

I am writing this book because I think people need to know what the Bible actually says about the god that Jews, Christians, and Muslims worship. Yes, that is correct. According to the Holy Book's narrative of those three religions, they all worship the god of Abraham despite referring to him by different names. The Jews generally refer to him as Yahweh; the Christians, as Jehovah or Jesus; and the Muslims, as Allah.

Most people in general are not aware that the Old Testament in the Christian Bible is also the Jewish Bible called the Tanakh, which is why the Bible is formally called the Judeo-Christian Bible. All three religions—Judaism, Christianity, and Islam—also share many of the same characters in their religious scriptures, such as the prophets Moses, Joshua, and Elijah. They also share the archangels Gabriel and Michael; all found in the Judeo-Christian Bible and the Islamic holy book Koran. These three religions are like three branches from the same tree with the same roots.

Other similarities between Christianity, Judaism, and Islam are, they end their prayers with the word *amen*, all three are awaiting a savior, they all believe in an apocalyptic judgment day, they all have a version of the skullcap, and ironically, they all believe their god and religion is superior to all other gods and religions. Since their creation these three religions have had major historical influences on human societies around the world. The most significant similarity these three religions have is, they are all major influences in today's political, social, and economic world events.

It is the opinion of the author that religious leaders are generally hesitant to discuss the biblical scriptures quoted in this book because they either have not read them or have read them and choose to ignore them. This book is about the biggest conspiracy in human history. It is about the greatest deception of all time. It is about who or what the god of the Bible really is. It is about the behavior of this entity that makes himself god of Judaism, Christianity, and Islam. It is about the negative influence this perceived god has had and is having on our world today.

I will describe how the three aforementioned Abrahamic religions are the major reason why human societies have historically been stuck in a cycle of war, famine, and disease. I do not think it coincidental that war, famine, and disease are common themes throughout the Bible narrative as well as in documented human history. It is not coincidental that biblical scripture and European history parallel each other. An example of this is the similarity among the ideas of the Promised Land, Manifest Destiny, and jihad. All three religious doctrines promote war.

Among other things, this book will discuss the historical relationship between religion, politics, and money in forming the present sociopolitical and economic reality that most humans exist in today.

The Judeo-Christian Bible I use as reference for this book is a 2017 copy of the King James Version that includes the Apocrypha and the book of Enoch. I mention this because not all Bibles are worded exactly the same though the overall narratives are basically the same. Many of these scriptures are considered grammatically incorrect by today's standards, but I did not make any corrections because I want to present them in their original form. I do, however, sometimes paraphrase in order to clarify the narrative.

Despite the many opinions of the origination of the biblical writings, this book is written not to agree or disagree with those opinions concerning translations from the original language or languages but to understand the English version as written.

The vast majority of Christians have never read the entire Bible. That is an absolute fact. I am sixty-three years old, and at this moment, I do not know anyone other than myself who has read the entire Bible from cover to cover. Those who have read or attempted to read the Judeo-Christian Bible from cover to cover realized that it can be very tedious reading.

Very little research has been done regarding those that have read the entire Bible. I have known many Bible readers, but none that have read it from cover to cover. Those who are familiar with some of the narratives and concepts in the Bible have generally obtained that information from listening to priests, ministers, and other religious leaders and by reading passages they have been directed to by those same religious leaders. Most people who read or have read the Bible already had preconceived ideas about the book before they began reading it. These preconceived ideas may include things such as the Bible is the Word of God, the Bible is the good book, the Bible is a holy book, the Bible is a way to communicate with God, and the Bible offers guidance in one's personal life. There are those that believe all Bible scripture can be interpreted to have a variety of meaning, so we need a professional clergy to interpret it for us. There are those who view the Bible as being a type of book of poetry.

Many people turn to the Bible in times of personal tragedy or conflict in their lives. This is why there are many converts for Christianity and Islam to be had in the US military and prison systems.

Note: Throughout most of this writing, I use a lowercase *g* for God to emphasize the fact that the god of the Judeo-Christian Bible is just one of countless gods in documented human history. I also mostly use the name Jehovah in referring to the same character because it is one of the names given to Moses when they first met in the book of Exodus. This God character in Exodus 3:14 told Moses his name was "I AM THAT I AM" and then, in the same conversation, told Moses to tell the Israelites that his name is "I AM."

In Exodus chapter 6:2–3, this same character refers to himself with three more names during another conversation with Moses: "And God spake unto Moses, and said unto him, I am the Lord. And I appeared unto Abraham, unto Isaac, and unto Jacob, by the name of God Almighty, but by my name JEHOVAH was I not known to them." Note that in the Koran, this same character is called Allah.

I have taken a practical approach in paraphrasing the English translation of biblical scripture. For example, when the scripture says, "The Lord is a man of war: the Lord is his name," I interpret this to mean that the biblical god Jehovah is a man who is occupied with war.

In Hosea 13:16, it says, "Samaria shall become desolate; for she hath rebelled against her God: they shall fall by the sword: their infants shall be dashed to pieces, and their women with child shall be ripped up." In plain English, this scripture is saying, Samaria will be destroyed for rebelling against Jehovah. This destruction will include tearing infants to pieces and ripping up pregnant women.

In Psalm 137:9, it says, "Happy shall he be, that taketh and dasheth thy little ones against the stone." In plain English, whoever takes little children and kills them by dashing them against a rock or stone will be happy.

In Numbers 31:17–18, it says, "Now therefore kill every male among the little ones, and kill every woman that hath known man by lying with him. But all the women children, that have not known a man by lying with him, keep alive for yourselves." It is clear that in this scripture, Jehovah, the god of the Bible, is ordering all the male children to be murdered along with all the nonvirgin females. He tells the Israelite warriors that they may keep all the virgin female children for themselves for slaves, wives, or concubines (Cohen, 2013).

The biggest mistake most people make concerning their belief in biblical scripture is they base their belief on someone else's interpretation. They are like the child who can't read and has to depend on someone else to read and interpret for them.

If one reads the description and especially the behavior of the god of the Judeo-Christian Bible with an unbiased mind and exercises a bit of critical thinking, it becomes obvious that he is the opposite of what we have been indoctrinated into believing. If you are a dogmatic, noncritical-thinking individual who insists on isolating yourself from other points of view, then I suggest you stop reading now so you might avoid being offended. Otherwise, my wish is that this book will be of help to you and others seeking truth because your love of the truth will help you set yourself free. This book was written with love, truth, and freedom in mind, heart, and soul.

CHAPTER 1

THE GOD OF THE BIBLE

Section 1
The Bible Says There Are More Than One God

In the book of Genesis 1:26, we read, "And God said, Let us make man in our image, after our likeness."

Who or what is this God of the Judeo-Christian Bible, and who is with him? The narrative is inferring that God is not by himself, but he is with other entities. They are going to make man in their image. The inference is that man already exists and that they (God and his companions) are going to make him more like themselves. God is already using the term *man* before he and his companions make him in their image and likeness because man already exists. A description of God is given in Exodus 15:3, "The Lord is a man of war: the Lord is his name." In other words, God and his companions are men who are going to make the existing man more like themselves. This is much like the European American attempting to acculturate or Americanize the indigenous Native Americans into the white American culture during the late 1800s in US history.

According to the biblical timeline, man was created approximately six thousand years ago (Valkanet, 2010). If this god and his accomplices made man in their image and after their likeness, as the Bible says, then let us look at their image and likeness, which is us humans.

There are arguably four major subraces that comprise the human race. There are many race categorization models to choose from when categorizing humans into race groups. However, according to DNA research, human DNA is 99.9 percent identical among all humans (Highfield, 2019). According to Wikipedia online, the shortest human ever officially documented in recent history stood one foot, nine and one-half inches tall. The tallest human stood eight feet, eleven inches tall, that is, 500 percent taller. Other variations among humans include but are not limited to skin color, hair, facial features, and other physical variations. How many God entities were there in Genesis that had a hand in making humans in their image? We see references to other gods throughout the Bible. For example:

Exodus 23:32—the primary god of the Bible, Jehovah, gives the following command: "Thou shalt make no covenant with them, nor with their gods."

Jehovah is commanding the Israelites to not make any agreements with other people nor their gods. There are obviously other gods other than Jehovah interacting with humans.

Exodus 23:13—"And make no mention of the name of other gods, neither let it be heard out of thy mouth."

Jehovah obviously doesn't want the Israelites to interact nor be influenced by any of the other gods.

Exodus 15:11—"Who is like unto thee, O Lord, among the gods?"

Second Kings 17:31—"And the Sepharvites burnt their children in fire to Adrammelech and Anammelech, the gods of Sepharvaim."

Here the narrator has named two of the other gods Adrammelech and Anammelech.

Judges 11:24—"Wilt not thou possess that which Chemosh thy god giveth thee to possess?"

Chemosh is another one of Jehovah's rival gods.

Names of some of the other gods mentioned in the Bible are Molech, Baal, Bel, and Dagon. It is interesting to note that the main god of the Bible, the one spelled with a capital *G* is called by many names such as God, GOD, I AM, I AM THAT I AM, Jehovah, JAH, Lord, Yahweh, Jesus, and many more names. Muslims refer to this same god as Allah.

In Exodus 3:1–14, Jehovah introduces himself to Moses when he speaks to him from inside a light in a bush in the desert in Egypt. He gives his name as I AM THAT I AM then tells Moses to tell the Israelites that his name is I AM and that he will be working through Moses for their benefit. Three chapters later, in Exodus 6:3, God says his name is Jehovah. Then in Exodus 6:7, this same man who has already been referring to himself as God says to Moses, "I will be to you as a God." Soon after, in Exodus 7:1, he says to Moses, "I have made thee a god to Pharaoh: and Aaron thy brother shall be thy prophet."

To clarify, according to the above biblical narrative, Jehovah makes himself as a god to Moses with Moses as his prophet. He then makes Moses as a god to Pharaoh with Aaron as his prophet. That's a pretty simple hierarchy of authority being created there.

Section 2
The God of the Judeo-Christian Bible Is a Man

The Bible says that the god Jehovah is a man. This is stated directly and indirectly in various sections of the Old Testament. For example, Exodus 15:3, "The Lord is a man of war: the Lord is his name." In Genesis 32: 24–30, there is an incident that shows Jehovah to be a man who wrestles with another man named Jacob whom he loses to. He then changes Jacob's name to Israel. The key point here is that the Bible says God is a man.

From Genesis 32:24–30, "And Jacob was left alone; and there wrestled a man with him until the breaking of the day . . . and the hollow of Jacob's thigh was out of joint, as he wrestled with him . . . And he said, Let me go, for the day breaketh. And he said, I will not let thee go, except thou bless me."

This interaction between the god Jehovah and Jacob emphasizes that Jehovah is a man who is physically wrestling with Jacob, who is also a man. Jehovah asks Jacob to let him go, but Jacob refuses to let him go until he blesses him. According to the narrative, Jacob had defeated Jehovah and had him at his mercy.

According to the biblical setting and description of God, Jehovah is but one of many so-called gods who is actually a man, which the biblical narrative focuses on to promote him as the primary god of the Bible. This begs the question, who wrote and to this day promotes the Judeo-Christian biblical narrative? The answer is men wrote and promote the Bible.

Another example that Jehovah is a man is found in Genesis 3:8, "And they heard the voice of the Lord God walking in the garden in the cool of the day: and Adam and his wife hid themselves from the presence of the Lord God amongst the trees of the garden." Note that they not only heard Jehovah's voice but he was also physically walking through the garden.

Another clue that Jehovah is a man is found in Genesis 6:9, "Noah was a just man and perfect in his generations, and Noah walked with God." In fact, Noah's great-grandfather named Enoch also walked with God, as written in Genesis 5:22–24:

> And Enoch walked with God after he begat Methuselah three hundred years, and begat sons and daughters. And all the days of Enoch were three hundred sixty and five years: And Enoch walked with God: and he was not; for God took him.

In other words, Enoch and Jehovah were physically interacting with each other for at least three hundred years. Jehovah then took Enoch when Enoch was 365 years old. Enoch did not "give up the ghost" or die before he was taken. This man referred to as God physically took Enoch somewhere while Enoch was still physically alive.

Other Bible verses inferring the main god of the Bible is a man described how he likes to eat what humans like to eat. For example, in Genesis 8:20–21: "And Noah builded an altar unto the Lord; and took of every clean beast, and of every clean fowl, and offered burnt offerings on the altar" (sounds like grilled meat). "And the Lord smelled a sweet savour" (smells and probably tastes like grilled meat).

Section 3
The God Jehovah Wants His Meals Prepared
a Certain Way at a Certain Time

In the book of Exodus, we find another glaring example that Jehovah is actually a man who enjoys eating and drinking like any other man of that time and place. He gives specific instructions on how he wants his lamb meat cooked with wine on the side: "The one lamb thou shalt offer in the morning, and the other lamb thou shalt offer at even.[1] And with the one lamb a tenth deal[2] of flour mingled with the fourth part of an hin[3] of beaten oil; and the fourth part of an hin of wine for a drink offering. And the other lamb thou shalt offer at even, and shalt do thereto according to the meat offering of the morning, and according to the drink offering thereof, for a sweet savour, an offering made by fire unto the Lord" (Exodus 29:39–41).

According to the above three verses, Jehovah wants to be fed once in the morning and again in the evening. He wants his lamb cooked by using the above recipe where a specific measurement of flour and oil is used; he also wants a certain amount of wine to wash it down with.

Section 4
Jehovah Specifies That He Does Not Want His
Fruit Cooked and Demands His Meat Salted

More biblical evidence that Jehovah has the same appetite for food as a person of that time and culture is found in Leviticus 2:12–13: "As for the oblation[4] of the firstfruits, ye shall offer them unto the Lord: but they shall not be burnt on the altar for a sweet savour. And every oblation of thy meat offering shalt thou season with salt; neither shalt

---

[1]   Evening
[2]   Approximately one gallon
[3]   1.5 gallons
[4]   A religious offering or sacrifice

thou suffer the salt of the covenant[5] of thy God to be lacking from thy meat offering: with all thine offerings thou shalt offer salt."

Jehovah gives specific instructions in the above two verses not to cook his fruit on the altar (grill) and that every piece of meat needs to be salted. He also reminds the Israelites that these specific cooking instructions are part of the covenant (contract) he has made with them.

Section 5
Jehovah Demands Baby Boys with His Ripe Fruit and Liquor

In Exodus 22:29, Jehovah reminds the Israelites to make sure that their offerings of ripe fruits, liquors, and their firstborn sons are not delayed. Apparently Jehovah has an appetite for liquor and firstborn male children. "Thou shalt not delay to offer the first of thy ripe fruits, and of thy liquors: the firstborn of thy sons shalt thou give unto me." Jehovah is giving the Israelites a stern reminder that they need to be on time in bringing him the first pickings of ripe fruit, liquor, and firstborn infant males.

It is obvious that Jehovah likes to eat ripe fruit and drink liquor. But what does he do with all the infant male children that the Israelites are forced to give him? The thought of offering infant children to Jehovah as oblations becomes more grotesque when we consider the fact that the words *offerings* and *oblations* are synonymous to the word *sacrifice*. It is obvious that the Israelites were being forced to give their infant sons to Jehovah along with feeding him meat, fruit, wine, and liquor. What does Jehovah do with these infant male children? Why is it so important to Jehovah that he obtains at least hundreds of male infant children at the same time he is obtaining food? Are they part of his choice of foods? Is he using them for other things besides food?

---

5   Contract or agreement

Section 6
Why Would God Need Money?

In Genesis 28:22, Jacob, who physically wrestled and defeated Jehovah, is planning on building a house for him. He promises Jehovah 10 percent of all his wealth for as long as he lives as written, "And this stone, which I have set for a pillar, shall be God's house: and of all that thou shalt give me I will surely give the tenth unto thee."

Question 1: If Jehovah is the supreme creator of all things, what need would he have of 10 percent of a man's wealth? Answer: He is not who he says he is; he is a fraud.

Question 2: Jacob physically wrestled and defeated Jehovah. He had Jehovah at his mercy and refused to release him until Jehovah blessed him. Does it not make more sense that Jehovah would be giving Jacob 10 percent of his wealth? Answer: Jacob can defeat Jehovah in hand-to-hand combat, but Jehovah has superior military technology at his disposal and, therefore, has made himself a god to Jacob who he renames Israel.

Section 7
Jehovah and His Angels Stop to Eat and Drink with Abraham on the Way to Destroy Sodom and Gomorrah

Genesis chapter 18 tells of an account where Abraham is sitting inside the entrance to his tent when Jehovah and two other men stopped to visit, drink, and eat with him on their way to destroy Sodom and Gomorrah. This account also reinforces the idea that Jehovah is a man as written in the following verses:

1. "And the Lord appeared unto him in the plains of Mamre: and he sat in the tent door in the heat of the day; and he lifted up his eyes and looked, and, lo, three men stood by him: and when he saw them, he ran to meet them from the tent door, and bowed himself toward the ground, and said, My Lord, if now I

have found favour in thy sight, pass not away, I pray thee, from thy servant: let a little water, I pray you, be fetched, and wash your feet, and rest yourselves under the tree. And I shall fetch a morsel of bread, and comfort ye your hearts . . . and Abraham hastened into the tent unto Sarah, and said, Make ready quickly three measures of fine meal, knead it, and make cakes upon the hearth. And Abraham ran unto the herd, and fetch a calf tender and good, and gave it unto a young man; and he hasted to dress it. And he took butter, and milk, and the calf which he had dressed, and set it before them; and he stood by them under the tree, and they did eat" (Genesis 18:1–8).

2. "And the men rose up from thence, and looked toward Sodom: and Abraham went with them to bring them on the way" (Genesis 18:16).

3. "And the Lord said, Because the cry of Sodom and Gomorrah is great, and because their sin is very grievous; I will go down now, and see whether they have done altogether according to the cry of it, which is come unto me; and if not, I will know. And the men turned their faces from thence, and went toward Sodom: but Abraham stood yet before the Lord" (Genesis 18.20–22). At this point, Abraham attempts to talk the Lord from destroying Sodom and Gomorrah.

4. "And the Lord went his way, as soon as he had left communing with Abraham: and Abraham returned unto his place" (Genesis 18:33).

In the above account, the narrator refers to the Lord (Jehovah) and his two companions as three men. Jehovah is traveling with two other men, and Abraham runs out to meet them. Abraham offers them water to wash their feet and something to eat, which they accept.

It is clear that Jehovah and his two companions are men because they are walking, washing their feet, eating, drinking, and holding informal face-to-face conversation with Abraham, which also indicates they speak the same language. Jehovah and his two companions are on their way to inspect the cities of Sodom and Gomorrah to see if they are as bad as reported. He is then going to make a decision on whether to destroy them or not.

Genesis chapter 19 describes the outcome of Jehovah's decision concerning Sodom and Gomorrah. According to the narrative, Jehovah sends two angels (men) to destroy the cities as written in Genesis 19:13 and 19:24, respectively, "For we will destroy this place, because the cry of them is waxen great before the face of the Lord; and the Lord hath sent us to destroy it" and "Then the Lord rained upon Sodom and upon Gomorrah brimstone and fire from the Lord out of heaven."

It stands to reason that the two angels Jehovah sent to destroy the cities were the same two men that were with Jehovah when they stopped and ate at Abraham's home. They are also the same individuals who are referred to as two angels in Genesis 19:1. They seem to be on a reconnaissance mission before destroying the city. They are the same two individuals that strike some of the men of Sodom blind in self-defense after those men attempt to sexually force themselves on them (Genesis 19:11). These same two individuals who are originally referred to as angels are then referred to as men in Genesis: 19:12.

It stands to reason that Jehovah and the two men that Abraham fed and had a face-to-face conversation with in Genesis chapter 18 concerning the destruction of Sodom and Gomorrah were the same three men who rained brimstone and fire from the sky upon Sodom and Gomorrah. It also stands to reason that these men were in some type of aircraft to be able to rain down upon Sodom and Gomorrah's destruction from the sky.

Section 8
Jehovah Gives His Prophet a Narcotic Drink as a Mental Stimulus

In Second Esdras chapter 14, there is an account where the prophet Esdras asks Jehovah to send the Holy Ghost into him so he can write the history of the world. It is written in Second Esdras 14:22, "But if I have found grace before thee, send the Holy Ghost into me, and I shall write all that hath been done in the world since the beginning, which were written in thy law, that men may find thy path, and that they which will live in the latter days may live."

Jehovah tells Esdras to gather five writers and to tell the people he would not be available for forty days. Jehovah then gives Esdras a cup of orange-colored liquid that he drinks that stimulates him for the task at hand. He then speaks and the writers write, and in forty days, they write two hundred and four books.

What was in the cup that Jehovah gave the prophet Esdras to drink in order to write 204 books in 40 days? Esdras said that the color of the liquid was like fire, which would make it an orange-colored liquid. How is the Holy Ghost that Jehovah sends into Esdras connected to the orange liquid that he drank? It stands to reason that the Holy Ghost experience is brought on by the orange liquid, which is actually a mind-altering substance. The account may be read in Second Esdras 14:36–48. The following is an excerpt from the account:

> In forty days they wrote two hundred and four books. And it came to pass, when the forty days were filled, that the Highest spake, saying, The first that thou hast written publish openly, that the worthy and unworthy may read it: But keep the seventy last, that thou mayest deliver them only to such as be wise among the people: For in them is the spring of understanding, the fountain of wisdom, and the stream of knowledge. And I did so.

It seemed that Jehovah gave these six guys some mind-altering substance, which motivated Esdras to verbalize his thoughts and motivated the five writers to write down the information dictated by Esdras. The information was then made into 204 books. The first 134 books were made available to everyone, but the last 70 were made available only to certain people.

Why are the last 70 books only available to certain individuals? Is this the beginning of secret societies? This brings to mind the fruit from the tree of knowledge of good and evil and the tree of life being only available to the gods in the Garden of Eden account.

Another account of the Holy Ghost is given in the New Testament in the book of Matthew. When Mary, the future mother of Jesus, was engaged to Joseph, the Holy Ghost made her pregnant with Jesus as written in Matthew 1:18, "Now the birth of Jesus Christ was on this wise: When as his mother Mary was espoused to Joseph, before they came together, she was found with child of the Holy Ghost."

Christianity teaches that the Holy Ghost is a third of the Christian godhead of the Father, Son, and Holy Ghost. In other words, their god Jehovah is made up of Jehovah (Father), Jesus (Son), and the Holy Ghost. Before impregnating Mary, Jehovah had also impregnated the following five women of the Old Testament: Sarah, Rebekah, Rachel, Manoah's wife (name not given), and Hannah. It stands to reason that the Holy Ghost is just another part of the deceptive manipulations presented by the men who concocted the god of the Bible.

So Mary is made pregnant with Jesus by the Holy Ghost. How did the Holy Ghost get Mary pregnant? It stands to reason that it happened in one of the following three possibilities:

1. *Sexual intercourse.* As mentioned throughout this book, Jehovah is a man or a manlike entity. If this is the case, he may have had sexual intercourse with Mary as his sons had sex with women in Genesis 6:2 and 6:4, "That the sons of God saw the daughters of men that they were fair; and they took them wives of all which they chose." and "There were giants in the earth in those days; and also after that, when the sons of God came in unto the daughters of men, and they bare children to them." Apparently, Jesus is just one of the many sons of the god Jehovah.

2. *Artificial insemination.* Sarah, Rebekah, Rachel, Manoah's wife, and Hannah had been infertile until Jehovah impregnated them. Artificial conception is not an unreasonable probability when taking into account the advanced technology inferred throughout the Bible.

3. *Made-up fantasy*—There are those that will explain the event as some type of mysterious, magical happening that we do not understand because we are not yet worthy, so we need to

have faith that the account happened as explained by today's religious authorities. This explanation follows the same logic and reasoning as the dogmatic tale of Santa Claus and how he makes the Christmas gifts at his shop in the North Pole, loads them on his sleigh pulled by flying reindeer, and personally delivers them to over a billion people all over the planet in one night. Not to mention the Easter Bunny hopping around with a basket full of colored chicken eggs and the tooth fairy leaving a quarter under your pillow in exchange for your old tooth. Children eventually figure out that the Santa story was made up for entertainment and to influence their behavior but continue passing on the same tale to their children. The story of the conception and birth of the Christmas Jesus plays a similar role for adults. All these stories are fueled by religious dogma, culture, and economics.

Section 9
Jehovah Compares Israel to a Fornicating Whore

In Ezekiel chapter 16, Jehovah compares his chosen people in Israel to a fornicating whore. He describes Israel as a naked young woman that he found, which he then clothed, nurtured, fell in love with, and married. He describes how beautiful she was and how he adorned her with luxurious clothing and jewelry. He says she became a whore that began fornicating with gods from other cultures by sacrificing her children to them. He then describes how in his jealousy and rage he is going to punish his wife Israel by turning her lovers against her where they will stone her and thrust her through with swords

In Ezekiel chapter 23, Jehovah tells his prophet Ezekiel what could be described as a pornographic allegory. In this allegory, he describes Jerusalem and Samaria as two of his wives who were sisters who became whores. He describes how they lusted over various men and had sex with them. He describes some of their lovers as having penises like donkeys and ejaculating like horses. He then describes how he is going to express his jealousy by turning their lovers against them to punish them with extreme violence. The following are excerpts from this allegory:

> Son of man, there were two women, the daughters of one mother: And they committed whoredoms in Egypt; they committed whoredoms in their youth: there were their breasts pressed, and there they bruised the teats of their virginity . . . Thus were their names; Samaria is Aholah, and Jerusalem Aholibah" (Ezekiel 23:1–4). "And the Babylonians came to her into the bed of love, and they defiled her with their whoredom" (Ezekiel 23:17). "For she doted upon her paramours,[6] whose flesh[7] is as the flesh of asses, and whose issue[8] is like the issue of horses" (Ezekiel 23:20). "And I will set my jealousy against thee, and they shall deal furiously with thee" (Ezekiel 23:25).

In the above allegory, Jehovah is personified as the righteous do-gooder who is wronged by the two young women he had taken pity on and married. They ended up acting like whores, so he manipulated their lovers to brutalize them as punishment for their behavior.

Section 10
Jehovah Thinks of Earth as His Footstool

Based on the following scripture, Jehovah doesn't think much of Mother Earth, "Thus saith the Lord, The heaven is my throne, and the earth is my footstool" (Isaiah 66:1).

---

6   Lovers

7   Penis

8   Ejaculation

CHAPTER 2

LACK OF MORALITY AND INTEGRITY

Section 1
Lots of Incest and Inbreeding Occurs in Biblical Scripture

According to biblical scripture there was much incest and inbreeding among the group of people who are considered the patriarchs of the religions Judaism, Christianity, and Islam.

In Genesis 19:30–38, Abraham's nephew Lot got drunk and had sex with his two daughters and made them pregnant, and they each gave birth to a son. One had a son named Moab, known as father of the Moabites, and the other had a son named Ammon, known as father of the Ammonites.

In Genesis 20:12, Abraham admitted that his wife Sarah was his half sister. He couldn't make her pregnant, so Jehovah made her pregnant instead, and she had a son named Isaac. Isaac then married his first cousin Rebekah, whom Jehovah also had to make pregnant because Isaac could not. She gave birth to a son named Jacob, whom Jehovah will later change to the name Israel. Then Jacob and his brother, Esau, each married their first cousins. Jacob married Leah and Rachel who are sisters. He could not get Rachel pregnant, so Jehovah again stepped in as he had done with Jacob's grandfather Abraham and father Isaac and made her pregnant with a son they named Joseph. Jacob, or Israel, eventually had twelve sons from four different wives. Each son then became the patriarch of his own tribe, hence the twelve tribes of Israel. Israel's oldest son, Reuben, had sex with one of his father's wives named Bilah.

The three major Abrahamic religions of Judaism, Christianity, and Islam all consider Abraham and Moses to be major patriarchs of their religions. Did you know that the birth of Moses was a result of incest and inbreeding? Moses and his brother Aaron were conceived after their father married their grandfather's sister, their father's biological aunt, as written in Exodus 6:20, "And Amram took him Jochebed his father's sister to wife; and she bare him Aaron and Moses."

Section 2
Jehovah and Moses Promote Pedophilia

As part of the many raids of murder and plunder commanded by Jehovah through Moses, the Israelite soldiers were ordered to kill all the male children but to take the female virgin children for themselves. For example, in Numbers 31:17–18, Jehovah commands Moses to order his men to do commit the following atrocities, "Now therefore kill every male among the little ones, and kill every woman that hath known man by lying with him. But all the women children that have not known a man by lying with him, keep alive for yourselves."

Religious scholars such as Shaye J. D. Cohen and Wil Gafney, PhD, agree that Moses instructs his soldiers that they may keep all the prepubescent female children as wives and for their sexual pleasure. Having sexual intercourse with female children as young as three years old was legal among the ancient Israelites (Discover the Truth, 2013).

The Old Testament is the Christian version of the Jewish bible Tanakh. An English version translated by Rabbi A.J. Rosenberg including commentary by the respected Jewish scholar of the Middle Ages Rabbi Shlomo Yitzchaki (aka Rashi 1040-1105), can be found on the Jewish website Chabad.ORG. According to Rosenberg and Rashi's commentary, Abraham's son Isaac, the one who he almost sacrificed, married Rebecca when she was three years old. Rebecca was born when

Isaac was thirty-seven years old. Rashi cites from Gen. Rabbah 57:1 "He waited for her until she would be fit for marital relations—three years—and then he married her" (Rosenberg 2019).

Much has been written throughout history concerning adults marrying children. Various researchers and religious scholars agree and disagree on practically every account concerning this topic. For example, it is said that the prophet Muhammed married a nine year old girl named Aisha. Some scholars disagree while others agree with this alleged historical fact. Agreement or disagreement of alleged historical facts seem to always be based on not just interpretation of historical writings but also on acceptance or rejection of these same historical writings whatever they may be. Some of the children in some of these writings are alleged to be as young as two years and some are said to be male children married to female adults. Examples of these alleged marriages may be found in the following website: muslimprophets. com/article.php?aid=35. There are many more websites that include referenced sources throughout the internet discussing the same topic.

This brings us back to the firstborn male children who Jehovah demands with his fruit and liquor from the Israelites in Exodus 22:29: "Thou shalt not delay to offer the first of thy ripe fruits, and of thy liquors: the firstborn of thy sons shalt thou give unto me."

What does·he do with these infant male children?

A clue to one of the probabilities of what may eventually have happened to these firstborn sons of the Israelites that they give to Jehovah is found over twenty-one hundred years later in the following account described by Rabbi Nuchem Rosenberg. He is a member of Brooklyn's Satmar Hasidim fundamentalist branch of Orthodox Judaism. The following is an excerpt from a news article of a description of what he witnessed:

> On a visit to Jerusalem in 2005, Rabbi Rosenberg
> entered into a mikvah (ritual Jewish bathhouse) in one
> of the holiest neighborhoods in the city, Mea She'arim.
> 'I opened a door that entered into a *schvitz* (sauna).
> Vapors everywhere, I can barely see. My eyes adjust,

and I see an old man, my age, long white beard, a holy-looking man, sitting in the vapors. On his lap, facing away from him, is a boy, maybe seven years old. And the old man is having anal sex with this boy.'

Rabbi Rosenberg paused, gathered himself, and went on: 'This boy was speared on the man like an animal, like a pig, and the boy was saying nothing. But on his face—fear. The old man looked at me without any fear, as if this was common practice. He didn't stop. I was so angry, I confronted him. He moved the boy from his penis, and I took the boy aside. I told this man, it is a sin before God, a *mishkovzucher*. What are you doing to this boy's soul? You're destroying this boy! He had a sponge on a stick to clean his back, and he hit me across the face with it. 'How dare you interrupt me!' he said.

I had heard of these things for a long time, but now I had seen'" (Ketcham, 2013).

The pedophile rapist strikes Rabbi Rosenberg across the face with authority for interrupting his raping of the young boy. This pedophile obviously believes he is doing nothing wrong. Why is that? It stands to reason he believes that homosexual pedophilia is good because his god Yahweh/Jehovah approves it and probably practiced it himself, hence, his demand that all the firstborn sons be given to him along with food and liquor.

The pedophile rapist in the bathhouse is probably a rabbi himself because according to Rabbi Rosenberg, this same pedophile was also part of the *mishmeres hatznuis*, the archconservative Orthodox modesty squad that regulates—often through threats of violence—proper moral conduct and dress in the relations between men and women. Note that this pedophile degenerate, like his god Yahweh/Jehovah, hypocritically preaches religious morals with the threat of violence for breaking these morals.

Where were the parents of the young boy while he was being raped by the religious authority? According to the above news article, when the father of the seven-year-old boy whom Rabbi Rosenberg rescued from the Jerusalem bathhouse showed up to pick up his son, he couldn't believe his son had been raped. "Trembling, terrified, he whisked his son away to get medical help but was still too scared to raise a formal complaint." They are taught that it is more sinful to talk about the abuse than the abuse itself.

Because of his disclosure of pedophilia within the aforementioned Jewish community, Rabbi Rosenberg had received death threats on a regular basis. He was charged by the "modesty squad" (the group that the old man who sodomized the young boy in the bathhouse was a member of) for the crime of having previously been seen walking down the street in Jerusalem with a married woman. He was referred to by self-described "great rabbis and rabbinical judges of the city of New York" as a "stumbling block for the House of Israel." Rabbi Rosenberg alleged that approximately half of the young males in Brooklyn's Hasidic community—the largest in the United States and one of the largest in the world—have been sexually assaulted by their elders (Ketcham, 2013).

The Catholic Church also has a history of pedophilia among its leaders. In 1531, Martin Luther claimed that Pope Leo X had vetoed a measure that cardinals should restrict the number of boys they kept for their (sexual) pleasure, "otherwise it would have been spread throughout the world how openly and shamelessly the Pope and the cardinals in Rome practice sodomy" (Wilson, 2007). According to a 2004 research study by the John Jay College of Criminal Justice for the United States Conference of Catholic Bishops, 4,392 Catholic priests and deacons in active ministry between 1950 and 2002 have been plausibly (neither withdrawn nor disproven) accused of underage sexual abuse by 10,667 individuals. On May 13, 2017, Pope Francis acknowledged that the Vatican had a two-thousand-case backlog of sex abuse cases (Wikipedia, Catholic Church sexual abuse cases, 2018).

The following headlines are from the *Washington Times* newspaper dated June 29, 1989: HOMOSEXUAL PROSTITUTION INQUIRY ENSNARES

VIPs with Reagan, Bush 'call boys' took midnight tour of White House. The following is an excerpt from the article:

> In addition to credit-card fraud, the investigation is said to be focused on illegal interstate prostitution, abduction and use of minors for sexual perversion, extortion, larceny and related illicit drug trafficking and use by prostitutes and their clients.

For those that are unaware, Ronald Reagan was the US president and George H. W. Bush was his vice president at the time of this incident. I wonder where they were when this was happening.

In April 1978, US congressman Fred Richmond was arrested for soliciting sex from a sixteen-year-old boy (Rudin, 1998).

On February 1, 1989, an Ohio TV station aired a videotape of a confrontation between US congressman Donald "Buz" Lukens and the mother of a teenage girl. The mother accused Lukens of paying her daughter to have sex with him since she was thirteen years old (Rudin, 1998).

There are many stories alleging former and present US politicians being involved in pedophilia, too many to mention in this book. Just recently, a convicted pedophile named Jeffrey Epstein was again charged with sex trafficking and sex trafficking conspiracy involving girls as young as fourteen years old (Spargo, 2019). Many high-profile people have been associated with him in that they socialized with him and traveled on his private passenger jet known as the Lolita Express, an alleged hot spot for underage sex orgies. Two of those passengers were allegedly former US president Bill Clinton and current US president Donald Trump (Prestigiacomo, 2016).

A June 11, 2013 *NBC News* report stated that investigations into alleged prostitution and pedophilia involving US State department officials were allegedly obstructed and covered up by then secretary of state Hillary Clinton (YouTube, 2019).

The sexual deviant behavior of some of today's world religious and political leaders should come as no surprise when we consider the historical leadership of their respective institutions.

Section 3
Rachel Prostitutes Her Husband, Jacob,
for a Drug Called Mandrake

Mandrake root is a hallucinogenic narcotic. It is used for various purposes such as witchcraft, inducing conception, and anesthesia. In Genesis 30:14–16, Jacob's second wife, Rachel, offered to Jacob's first wife, Leah—who is also her sister—sex with Jacob for some mandrake that Leah's son Reuben had found in the fields. Apparently, Jacob had been ignoring his first wife, Leah, and preferred sleeping with her sister, Rachel, because she was younger and more beautiful, but she was also unable to conceive. At this time, Leah had already given birth to three sons, and Rachel was desperate to conceive for the first time, hence her desire for mandrake root as written in Genesis 30:14–16:

> And Reuben went in the days of wheat harvest, and found mandrakes in the field, and brought them unto his mother Leah. Then Rachel said to Leah, Give me, I pray thee, of thy son's mandrakes. And she said unto her, Is it a small matter that thou hast taken my husband? And wouldest thou take away my son's mandrakes also? And Rachel said, Therefore he shall lie with thee tonight for thy son's mandrakes. And Jacob came out of the field in the evening, and Leah went out to meet him, and said, Thou must come in unto me; for surely I have hired thee with my son's mandrakes. And he lay with her that night.

Section 4
King David and His Sons Lack Moral Character

King David is probably the most famous of all the kings of Israel. He is best known for killing the giant Goliath, being the father of King Solomon, and being part of the bloodline of Abraham and Jesus as mentioned in the Gospel of Matthew. He also paid two hundred Philistine foreskins to King Saul as payment for marrying his daughter, which would be his first of hundreds of wives (First Samuel 18:27).

An example of King David's moral character, or lack thereof, is shown in Second Samuel chapters 11–12. In this account, Uriah was one of King David's most trusted generals. David saw the general's wife bathing as he was looking out from his roof. He had her sent to him and had sex with her, resulting in her becoming pregnant. He then sent her husband, Uriah, to the most dangerous part of the battlefield, hoping that he would be killed so he could marry his wife. His plan succeeded as General Uriah was killed in battle. After his general was killed, King David married his widow as planned.

Apparently, Jehovah did not approve of what David did but instead of going directly to David, he contacted Nathan the prophet and told him of his disapproval. The prophet Nathan then communicated Jehovah's disapproval to King David. To punish King David, Jehovah killed the child who was born to him and General Uriah's widow by inflicting it with a disease. This account in Second Samuel chapters 11 and 12 not only showed King David's lack of moral character but Jehovah's as well in that he murdered an innocent infant to punish a corrupt, immoral adult.

Examples of the lack of moral character in the sons of King David were presented in Second Samuel chapter 13. Absalom and Amnon were both sons of King David. They had a virgin sister named Tamar whom Amnon sexually desires. Amnon developed a plan in order to seduce his sister. He pretended to be sick, and the king went to visit him. Amnon then made a request that the king send his sister, Tamar, to take care of him while he was sick, and King David granted his request.

When Tamar went to her brother Amnon's house, he sent everyone away so he could be alone with her and then raped her even though she begged him not to. After he raped her, he felt much hate for her and sent her away. This account may be read in Second Samuel 13:8–19.

The biblical narrative goes on to say when King David found out what happened, he became very angry. However, there were no consequences for his son Amnon. The narrative suggested that King David would have approved of a sexual relationship between his son and his daughter if his son Amnon would have formally requested it. Tamar's other brother Absalom then decided to kill his brother Amnon for raping their sister. It took him two years to carry out his plan. Absalom invited all his brothers, including Amnon, to a gathering and instructed his servants to wait until Amnon gets drunk and then killed him as written in Second Samuel 13:28–29:

> Now Absalom had commanded his servants, saying, Mark ye now when Amnon's heart is merry with wine, and when I say unto you, Smite Amnon, then kill him, fear not: have not I commanded you? Be courageous, and be valiant. And the servants of Absalom did unto Amnon as Absalom had commanded. Then all the king's sons arose, and every man gat him up upon his mule, and fled.

Such is the immoral behavior of King David and his sons. Amnon the rapist could have had sex with any woman in the kingdom, but he chose to rape his sister instead. His father, King David, also could have had sex with any woman in the kingdom, but instead, he chose to seduce the wife of his loyal general Uriah and then orchestrated his death in order to marry her. Absalom invited all his brothers, including the rapist Amnon, to a party for the specific purpose of murdering him. Instead of objecting to the murder of their brother that happened in their presence, King David's other sons all fled the murder scene.

Section 5
King David's Son Has Sex in Public with His Father's Wives

In Second Samuel 15–18, Absalom attempted to overthrow his father, King David, but failed. Nevertheless, tens of thousands of Israelites, including himself, were killed as a result. One of the things Absalom did that signified his immorality was when he had sex with his father's concubines/wives in public as written in Second Samuel 16:22, "So they spread Absalom a tent upon the top of the house; and Absalom went in unto his father's concubines in the sight of all Israel."

Section 6
Feud between the House of Saul and the House of David Is Similar to Mafia Wars

After the death of King Saul and when David became king, there was civil war among the Israelites between the house of David and the house of Saul. There were many Israelites who remained loyal to the house of Saul and his three sons. This led to political assassinations and clashes between the two groups. In Second Samuel chapter 4, there was an account where King David's men, without his approval, sneaked into the house of a rival named Ishbosheth, a son of the previous king Saul. They murdered him while he was lying in bed and then cut his head off and took it to King David. Ironically, instead of rewarding them, David had them killed, "And David commanded his young men, and they slew them, and cut off their hands and their feet, and hanged them up over the pool in Hebron" (Second Samuel 4:12).

Section 7
King David Lacked Sympathy for the Crippled and Blind

King David apparently had no sympathy for the crippled and blind as written in Second Samuel 5:8, "And David said on that day,

Whosoever getteth up to the gutter, and smiteth the Jebusites, and the lame and the blind, that are hated of David's soul, he shall be chief and captain. Wherefore they said, The blind and the lame shall not come into the house."

Section 8
According to Bible Scripture, King David and His Soldiers Destroyed Their Own Soul by Raping Other Men's Wives and Committing Adultery

Proverbs 6:32 says, "But whoso committeth adultery with a woman lacketh understanding: he that doeth it destroyeth his own soul." Throughout the Bible, Jehovah orchestrates the murder of helpless children and the rape of other men's wives. According to the Bible, these men destroyed their own souls by following Jehovah's commands. King David destroyed his own soul by having sex with his loyal general Uriah's wife.

Section 9
According to Scripture, Dashing Children against Stone Is Considered Happiness

A *psalm* is defined as "a sacred song or hymn" (Random House, 1992). The following is from the book of Psalm 137:9, "Happy shall he be, that taketh and dasheth thy little ones against the stones." Yes, this is written in the Bible word for word. This is considered a "sacred song or hymn," taking little babies and busting their heads open by slamming them against a stone wall. It just reemphasizes the evil, cowardly, and brutal behavior of Jehovah and the people who committed murder in his name.

It is common in the Old Testament as part of their military assaults that Jehovah orders the Israelites kill everyone including children and to rip up pregnant women. It is mind-boggling how such an evil description of cruelty can be regarded as sacred scripture.

CHAPTER 3

GOD OF AVARICE

Section 1
The Accumulation of Gold and Silver Is a Primary
Objective of the Biblical God Jehovah

Jehovah first expresses his desire for gold and silver in Exodus 11:2 at the beginning of the Israeli emigration from Egypt where he said, "Speak now in the ears of the people, and let every man borrow of his neighbor, and every woman of her neighbor, jewels of silver, and jewels of gold."

Numbers 31:50–54 presents a description of how Jehovah begins accumulating massive amounts of gold and silver: "We have therefore brought an oblation for the Lord, what every man hath gotten, of jewels of gold, chains, and bracelets, rings, earrings, and tablets, to make atonement for our souls before the Lord" and "And all the gold of the offering that they offered up to the Lord, of the captains of thousands, and of the captains of hundreds, was sixteen thousand seven hundred and fifty shekels"[9] (This is a little over one quarter ton of gold for the Lord Jehovah). This narrative is one of many examples of how Jehovah has the Israelites give him gold and jewels for their sins to be pardoned. This is similar to indulgences that were sold by the Roman

---

[9]   One shekel is approximately one half ounce

Catholic Church during the European Middle Ages. Indulgences were forgiveness of sins sold for money.

In Joshua 6:19, we see that all the gold, silver, and other precious metals being plundered by Jehovah and the Israelites are put into the treasury of Jehovah: "But all the silver, and gold, and vessels of brass and iron, are consecrated unto the Lord: they shall come into the treasury of the Lord."

Joshua 6:21 present another example of Jehovah using the Israelites in looting cities of their gold and silver and committing mass murder. He not only orders the murder of children, women, and men, but all their animals as well. "And they utterly destroyed all that was in the city, both man and woman, young and old, and ox, and sheep, and ass, with the edge of the sword."

Joshua 6:24, "And they burnt the city with fire, and all that was therein: only the silver, and the gold, and the vessels of brass and of iron, they put into the treasury of the house of the Lord."

Is it not interesting that Jehovah, the god of the Bible, has a treasury where the Israelites store all his gold, silver, and other precious metals? Jehovah becomes very wealthy by plundering other nations of their gold, silver, and other types of wealth. This again begs the question, If Jehovah is God, why does he desire gold and silver so much, and why does he manipulate one group of people to take it from another group and bring it to him? Perhaps it is because he is really just a thuggish, greedy, psychopathic man with access to superior military technology. We must keep in mind that he is described as a god of war.

Food for thought: a group of men today land in the Amazon jungle in a helicopter. These men are in possession of modern military technology. They are led by a brutish, greedy thug who decides to take advantage of the indigenous people whose military technology consists of wooden spears. He kills a few with his automatic weapon and eventually convinces them that he is their god from heaven. This self-proclaimed god terrorizes and inflicts the people with fear-based mind control in order to act out his psychopathic desires. After a while, he discovers that these people and the other tribes of the area possess and have access to gold and other types of wealth. He then manipulates the tribe that he has convinced that he is God to forcefully take the wealth from the surrounding tribes and bring it to him. He, of course, helps them easily defeat the other tribes by providing them with military assistance. This story parallels the story of Jehovah and the Israelites.

Section 2
Jehovah Has an Entire Family Brutally Murdered for Keeping Some Gold and Silver for Themselves

Joshua chapter 7 provides an example of how Jehovah dealt with someone attempting to keep some of the wealth taken in the looting of the city of Jericho. He not only killed the individual but also his entire family.

In the story, Jehovah had just led the prophet Joshua and the Israelites in destroying and taking all of Jericho's wealth. He was aware that one of the soldiers, named Achan, had kept a garment and some gold and silver from the acquired loot.

No one except Jehovah was aware of Achan's actions. However, instead of making Achan's actions known, Jehovah allowed the next raid to fail miserably where Joshua's soldiers were soundly defeated. Joshua was devastated and emotionally inquired of Jehovah why he allowed such a devastating defeat. Jehovah told Joshua that he allowed it because someone had broken his commandments. He told Joshua that he was not going to help him win any more battles until the individuals who stole from him were destroyed. He then had Joshua search each household from each tribe of Israel for the missing loot.

Jehovah had told Joshua that Achan was the guilty one before his household was searched, so Joshua implored Achan to confess to Jehovah what he had done. Achan, probably hoping that Jehovah will show him mercy, admitted his guilt and told Joshua that the stolen items were buried in the ground inside his tent. The items were promptly confiscated, and Achan and all his sons and daughters were brought before Joshua and Jehovah. As punishment, Achan and his sons and daughters were stoned and burned to death. The account can be read in its entirety in Joshua chapter 7.

By orchestrating the above events leading to the murder of Achan and his entire family, Jehovah is emphasizing the fear of God and total submission to him within the minds of the Israeli people. This helps ensure that they submit to him all the wealth that is taken from the other unfortunate people who are also victims of his insatiable desire for blood and wealth.

Section 3
Solomon's Temple Epitomizes Jehovah's Avarice

First Kings chapters 5–7 describes a house that King Solomon built for Jehovah. A massive amount of gold and silver was included in the construction of this house, which was also known as Solomon's Temple. The gold and silver used in the construction of the temple was taken from the peoples whom the Israelites murdered and plundered as described in the Old Testament.

In First Chronicles 22:14, King David is speaking to a young future king Solomon, "Now behold, in my trouble I have prepared for the house of the Lord an hundred thousand talents[10] of gold, and a thousand thousand talents of silver." In today's US units of measure, this is equivalent to 3,750 tons of gold and 37,500 tons of silver.

In First Chronicles 29:3–4, King David contributed another three thousand talents of gold and seven thousand talents of silver. That is, another 112 ½ tons of gold and 262 ½ tons of silver.

In First Chronicles 29:6–7, we see others in the Israeli government also contributing gold and silver for the construction of the temple.

The total amount of gold used in building Jehovah's house was approximately 4,050 tons and 40 pounds of gold. Total amount of silver used on the temple construction was 38,137 ½ tons.

---

[10] One talent weighs approximately 75 lbs.

After this house of the Lord was completed, King Solomon held a massive blood ritual in which so many animals were sacrificed they could not count them. "And king Solomon, and all the congregation of Israel, that were assembled unto him, were with him before the ark, sacrificing sheep and oxen, that could not be told nor numbered for multitude" (First Kings 8:5). This does not include sacrificing countless men, women, and children who were slaughtered in the process of accumulating the gold and silver used to build the house of the Lord, also known as King Solomon's Temple.

Section 4
The Leaders of the Early Christian Church Demand Members to Give All Their Wealth to the Church Leaders

In Acts 4:34–35, we find an example of the original Christian leaders and their method of accumulating wealth. They demand that all members give up their personal wealth to the new Jewish religion called Christianity. This wealth is then redistributed by the leaders. They are practicing the same demands as Jehovah of the Old Testament, who demanded gold, silver, and other types of wealth. In both cases, the religious leaders accumulate a massive amount of wealth and power for themselves at the expense of the general populace:

"Neither was there any among them that lacked: for as many as were possessions of lands or houses, sold them, and brought the prices of the things that were sold, And laid them down at the apostles' feet: and distribution was made unto every man according as he had need."

It is interesting how the above system sounds similar to communism. Like communism, the leaders grow rich, powerful, and oppressive at the expense of the general population. This is generally true of any modern political system, including capitalism.

Section 5
Jehovah Murders a Man and His Wife for Attempting to Keep Some of the Money Earned from Selling Their Land

New Testament Acts 5:1–11 presents an account of what happened to a man and his wife who did not submit their entire wealth to the new Christian Church. In the story, a man named Ananias and his wife, Sapphira, sold their land and donated part of the money to the church and kept the other part for themselves. The apostle Peter accused him and Satan of lying to God by not giving the full amount to the church. Ananias was killed immediately, and so was his wife when she also denied keeping part of the money received from selling their personal property.

According to the above scriptures, Jehovah killed a man and his wife for not giving the new Jewish organization, today known as the Roman Catholic Church, all the money they earned from selling their land. When reading the account in its entirety, it is truly insidious how the narrative attempts to put the guilt of committing evil (sin) on the husband and wife when, in fact, the apostle Peter and Jehovah are the ones committing the crimes of extortion and murder.

Section 6
Fear and Murder Are Common Themes in Jehovah's Accumulation of Wealth in Both the Old and New Testaments

Peter in the aforementioned account of Ananias and his wife, Sapphira, was the first pope of the Roman Catholic Church. Control and accumulation of wealth through fear and murder had historically been part of the machinations of the Jewish, Christian, and Islamic religions.

The New Testament accounts of extortion and murder by the early Christian church paralleled the account of Achan of Joshua chapter 7 in the Old Testament. Recall in the account that Jehovah and his prophet Joshua had Achan and his entire family stoned and burned to death because Achan had kept some of the items that he had helped Joshua and the other Israelites pillage from the inhabitants of the city of Jericho.

The accounts of Achan in the Old Testament and of Ananias and Sapphira in the New Testament are just two examples of the Jewish and Christian god Jehovah's pathological demand for wealth. Both accounts were apparently orchestrated by Jehovah to serve as a warning to the rest of the people that keeping wealth from him was a mortal sin punishable by death. In the Old Testament account, Jehovah could immediately have had Achan apprehended and punished. However, he instead chose to prolong the incident and had Achan and his entire family murdered as a lesson on why one should never keep anything from him, especially gold. In the New Testament account, Jehovah could have also allowed Ananias and Sapphira a second chance to submit their entire wealth, but he again chose to murder them as a warning to others about what happens when you do not submit your entire personal wealth to Jehovah.

These biblical accounts again beg the question, What about the all-merciful god? Jehovah is instead like the ruthless psychopathic mobster who says "Your money is my money, and my money is my money. Fuck with my money, and I will kill you!"

CHAPTER 4

JEHOVAH WANTS TOTAL MIND CONTROL OF HUMANITY

Section 1
The Bible Promotes Slavery

One would think that a just god would oppose the buying and selling of humans. However, instead of saying that slavery is wrong, biblical scripture teaches that the slaves should honor their masters and to not do so is considered a sin because it is a law of God and should not be broken as written in First Timothy 6:1, "Let as many servants as are under the yoke count their own masters worthy of all honour, that the name of God and his doctrine be not blasphemed."

A set of scriptures that promote slavery, fear, cruelty, and total submission to an unjust government are found in First Peter 2:17–19, "Honour all men. Love the brotherhood. Fear God. Honour the king.[11] Servants, be subject to your masters with all fear; not only to the good and gentle, but also to the froward.[12] For this is thankworthy, if a man for conscience toward God endure grief, suffering wrongfully."

---

[11] King is symbolic of government
[12] Mean and rough

In other words, everyone should fear God and honor the government because it represents God (divine right); therefore, the government should be feared as well. If you are a servant (slave), you should be especially fearful and submissive towards authority even if that authority is cruel and unjust.

Section 2
American Christian Hypocrisy Concerning
Freedom Is Historically Self-Evident

Ironically, in compliance with biblical scripture, chattel slavery[13] was becoming institutionalized in the United States during the same time that this new country was being perceived as a beacon of freedom by the rest of the world.

This institutionalization happened regardless of the ideas written in the US Declaration of Independence that all men are created equal and are born with the natural rights of "life, liberty, and the pursuit of happiness." This, of course, did not apply to the indigenous peoples in the path of US fulfillment of their version of the Old Testament Promised Land scenario where the American indigenous peoples were subjected to genocide and people of African descent were subjected to institutionalized chattel slavery.

The American slave masters, however, were eager to Christianize the black slaves in order to manipulate them into compliance with scriptures from the Bible concerning the relationship between slave and slave master. This included the false interpretation of scripture to justify using skin color as a basis for the type of slavery institutionalized in the United States. For example, some American Christian groups used their interpretation of biblical scripture concerning the curse of Ham in Genesis 9: 22-27 and the mark on Cain in Genesis 4:15 to justify the institutionalized enslavement of black people based on skin color.

---

[13] System of slavery where slaves are considered property similar to cattle

These interpretations include turning certain biblical characters' skin from white to black and condemning their descendants to perpetual slavery. Most American Christian groups segregated the blacks from the whites, and some would not allow blacks into the priesthood because of their skin color. The Mormon Church, for example, from 1849 to 1978, prohibited anyone with black ancestry from being ordained to the priesthood (Wikipedia, 2018).

The fact of the matter is there is no reference to skin color in any biblical scriptures regarding slavery. This is strictly a racist concept perpetuated by those in positions of power that economically benefitted from this false interpretation of biblical scripture. Ironically, the original Israelites of the Bible were dark-skinned people of African descent (Service, 2010).

Section 3
The Bible Is Full of Contradictions and Hypocrisy

The Bible says that humans are created in the image of Jehovah, yet humans are referred to as animals—that is, sheep, goats, dogs, etc. It says that Jehovah is truth, loves people, and wants people to be happy, but his treatment of people is full of deception, murder, torture, and oppression.

The truth is that Jehovah has kept truth from humanity and has been an obstacle to truth beginning with the story of the Garden of Eden. He places more value on gold and silver more than he does people. He demands total mental and physical control of people. He doesn't care whether people are happy or not as long as they obey him without question.

According to the books of Genesis and Exodus, God is a man. It is indicated that this man had control over the tree of knowledge and the tree of life in the allegory of Adam and Eve. Adam and Eve ate from the tree of knowledge, but the man called God/Jehovah kept them from eating from the tree of life preventing them from physically living forever. It stands to reason that Jehovah continues to have access to the tree of life and may still be physically alive today. Perhaps his control of the rest of humanity is being carried out through the governments that he has orchestrated into existence. Modern governments of the world today are part of his orchestration to maintain control of human civilization. The idea that these governments are controlled through secret organizations is not that far-fetched when we think about the story of Esdras and the books he wrote about the history of the world. Seventy of the 204 books he wrote were only allowed to be read by certain individuals, hence the start of secret societies.

Jehovah's laws are the Ten Commandments, which he and the governments influenced by him do not obey themselves, especially the commandments that say "thou shalt not kill" and "thou shalt not steal." His demands for blood sacrifice have continued up to the present in the guise of law enforcement, wars, and other types of killings. These crimes against humanity are orchestrated through corrupt criminal political systems, the three Abrahamic religions, and international banking systems. He attempts to destroy what he cannot control. Truth and freedom are his main targets. He preys on the weak and plots against the strong in his never-ending quest for total and complete control of humanity.

Jehovah, the self-appointed god of the Bible, wants humans to remain as children so they may look up to him as a small child looks up to his parent. This is inferred in Ephesians 5:1, "Be ye therefore followers of God, as dear children" and Ephesians 6:1, "Children, obey your parents in the Lord: for this is right."

In practicality, according to the biblical narrative, Jehovah is like the cruel, deceitful, abusive parent who wants to keep his children fearful and totally submissive to him. It is time for the children to grow up and realize what the god of the Bible really is.

Section 4
Jehovah Wants Humans Ignorant of the Reality They Exist In

Why would Jehovah in Genesis be so protective of the symbolic tree of knowledge and the tree of life? If we reason Adam and Eve to be a metaphor for humanity and the tree of knowledge and the tree of life to be metaphors for endless knowledge and immortality, it makes logical sense that Jehovah wanted to limit and control human access to both knowledge and life span.

Three specific examples given of what Jehovah wanted Adam and Eve (humans) to remain ignorant of are (1) they were naked, (2) the concept of good and evil, and (3) they can live forever.

As written in Genesis 3:7, after Adam and Eve had eaten from the tree of knowledge, "And the eyes of them both were opened, and they knew that they were naked; and they sewed fig leaves together, and made themselves aprons."

The above verse is inferring that humans were unaware of the reality they existed in. They became aware of that reality only after they ate from the tree of knowledge. Afterward, Adam and Eve hid from Jehovah as he was walking in the garden and they heard his voice. Jehovah then called out to Adam, and Adam responded, "I heard thy voice in the garden, and I was afraid, because I was naked; and I hid myself." Jehovah then responded, "Who told thee that thou wast naked? Hast thou eaten of the tree, whereof I commanded thee that thou shouldest not eat?" (Genesis 3:10–11)

Why was being naked a nonissue for Adam and Eve before eating from the tree of knowledge? It seemed that Jehovah had total control over their minds and wanted them to be naked but to be unaware of their nakedness. Was Jehovah also naked? Gaining knowledge made Adam and Eve aware that they in fact were naked, though Jehovah wanted to keep them ignorant of that fact in order to maintain control of their perception of reality. Jehovah lost the total mind and physical control he had over Adam and Eve (humans) after they gained knowledge.

Jehovah became concerned that Adam and Eve (humans) may become equal to him and the other gods after eating from the tree of knowledge. He was also concerned that they might eat from the tree of life and gain the ability to physically live forever and become more powerful than he and his god companions, as written in Genesis 3:22, "And the Lord God said, Behold, the man is become as one of us, to know good and evil: and now, lest he put forth his hand, and take also of the tree of life, and eat, and live forever."

Jehovah was so concerned with the probability that man will eat from the tree of life and live forever that he expelled Adam and Eve from the Garden of Eden and set up a security system to keep them away as written in Genesis 3:24, "So he drove out the man, and he placed at the east of the garden of Eden Cherubims[14], and a flaming sword which turned every way, to keep the way of the tree of life."

Why was Jehovah so concerned that humans would live forever? He did not want humans to physically live forever because he would lose the fear of death as a means of control over them.

Why was Jehovah so concerned that humans became aware of good and evil?

Humans are born with certain instincts as are any other life forms. What seems to separate humans from the rest of the animal kingdom is moral instinct and the idea of right and wrong and good and evil. In my opinion, humans are social entities naturally born with a moral compass that is necessary for living together in peace. Oppressive government interferes with natural morality and attempts to replace it with manufactured religious morals in its attempt at total control of the individual, hence Jehovah commanding total obedience to government even if it is cruel and oppressive (First Peter 2:17–19).

Perhaps Jehovah had stripped Adam and Eve of their moral instinct. I suggest that they began recovering this and other parts of their natural or instinctual knowledge when they began eating from the tree of knowledge. Jehovah became upset because he no longer had total control over them.

Section 5
Adam and Eve (Humans) Are Jehovah's Slaves
on the Plantation of the Garden of Eden

Jehovah wanting humans to remain ignorant of their reality parallels the reason why the slave masters in the United States wanted to keep their slaves ignorant. It was against Jehovah's law for humans to eat from

---

[14] A specific type of angels used as guards

the tree of knowledge for the same reason it was against the American slave masters' law to teach black slaves to read and write. The idea is that ignorant slaves are easier to control than are knowledgeable slaves.

I suggest humans existed as slaves on Jehovah's plantation called Eden but were unaware of the fact they were his slaves until eating from the tree of knowledge. They then became more knowledgeable and achieved a higher consciousness. Before this, they had been his mental and physical slaves. The general idea concerning the story of Adam and Eve is that they were happy in the Garden of Eden as long as they remained ignorant. Ignorance was bliss.

The best slaves are happy slaves who are ignorant to the fact that they are slaves and therefore have no desire to be free because they are unaware of what true freedom is. Such was the case concerning the slaves Adam and Eve (humanity) and Jehovah their slave master.

Section 6
Jehovah Decreases Human Life Span to
Ensure His Superiority over Them

The book of Genesis tells us Adam lived for 930 years; Seth, 912 years; Enos, 905 years; Cainan, 910 years; Mahalaleel, 895 years; Jared, 962 years; Methuselah, 969 years; Noah, 950 years; and Lamech, 777 years. The generations that followed progressively had a shorter life span. Shem lived 600 years; Arphaxad, 438 years; Salah, 433 years; Eber, 464 years; Peleg, 239 years; Reu, 239 years; Serug, 230 years; Nahor, 148; Abraham, 175 years; Isaac, 180 years; Joseph, 110 years; and Moses, 120 years. Today, life expectancy for humans varies from country to country. It ranges from approximately 32 years in Swaziland to 82 years in Japan (PRB 2014 and 2015 World Population Data Sheets 2019).

By shortening human life span, Jehovah was trying to ensure that humans would never live long enough to challenge his dominance of the physical world.

Section 7
Jehovah Does Not Want Humans to Unite and Live in Peace

Jehovah sees the peaceful, unified existence of humanity as a threat to his dominance of human society and the physical plane. He does not want humanity uniting, working together, and living in peace. This is demonstrated in the Tower of Babel account in Genesis chapter 11, "And the whole earth was of one language, and of one speech."

The inference here is that the people are united and living in peace. There are no wars. They then decide to build a city with a tower that will reach up into heaven (space exploration), which alarms Jehovah and his fellow gods, as you can read in the following verses:

> And the Lord came down to see the city and the tower, which the children of men builded. And the Lord said, Behold, the people is one, and they have all one language: and this they begin to do: and now nothing will be restrained from them, which they have imagined to do. Go to, let us go down, and there confound their language, that they may not understand one another's speech. So the Lord scattered them abroad from thence upon the face of all the earth and they left off to build the city (Genesis 11:5–8).

It is obvious that Jehovah is not a friend of humanity. He does not want man to unite and live as one people for the same reason he did not want the allegorical Adam and Eve to gain knowledge from the tree of knowledge nor increase their life span from the tree of life. His main objective is total control of humanity. Human access to unlimited knowledge, unlimited longevity, and living together in peace is an obstacle to Jehovah's total mind control agenda.

When Adam and Eve (humans) ate from the tree of knowledge, it was the beginning of their becoming conscious of the reality they were living in. Jehovah then made it a priority to keep them away from the tree of life to ensure their life span remained limited. Consequently, they would not have enough time to individually answer all their questions concerning their individual and collective earthly existence. Jehovah's greatest fear is people becoming aware of his true nature. People would then understand that he is like the cosmic parasite in Carlos Castaneda's book *The Active Side of Infinity* (Castaneda, 1998, pp. 218–20).

Concerning the Tower of Babel, the threat of humans becoming equal and perhaps superior to Jehovah and his accomplices (other gods) was great enough to have them come down and destroy the unity that existed among humans. It stands to reason that the destruction of this unity took a considerable amount of time and was orchestrated by Jehovah.

The Judeo-Christian Bible is full of examples of Jehovah orchestrating conflicts and divisions among humans. Using the systems of politics, money, and religion as his tools, he orchestrates wars between humans of the Old Testament where at least hundreds of thousands of men, women, and children are savagely slaughtered. It stands to reason that he has continued doing the same throughout modern history. A few examples of these wars are the Crusades, American and French Revolutions, US Civil War, World Wars I and II, Korean and Vietnam Wars, the Cold War, the war on drugs, the war on terror, and all other wars and so-called military conflicts happening today. I suggest that the man of war Jehovah is directly and indirectly responsible for approximately 100 percent of all military conflicts around the world today.

Section 8
Moses Initially Rejects the Leadership Role Assigned to Him by Jehovah

In Exodus chapters 3 and 4, Jehovah is recruiting Moses as the main actor in orchestrating the Israeli people's movement out of Egypt. He goes over the script, including showing Moses what appear to be magic tricks such as having him cast the rod he gave him on the ground where Jehovah turns it into a snake. Jehovah is going over the plan with Moses like a Hollywood movie director previewing a script with a leading actor. He also previews the part of the script where he will kill the firstborn of Egypt. Moses expresses reluctance in accepting the role Jehovah has chosen for him by making excuses such as the people will not listen to him because he is not a good speaker. He suggests to Jehovah that he find someone else to play his part, which makes Jehovah angry to the point where he decides to kill Moses but his wife intervenes and Jehovah changes his mind.

Section 9
Jehovah Orchestrates the Events of Exodus
by Hardening Pharaoh's Heart

In the book of Exodus, Jehovah manipulated Pharaoh to not let the Israelites leave Egypt by "hardening his heart" approximately thirteen times (Exodus 4:21, 7:13, 7:22, 8:15, 8:19, 8:32, 9:12, 9:34; 10:1, 10:20, 10:27, 11:10, 14:4). The result was an increase of pain and suffering especially among the Egyptians. For example, in Exodus chapter 9, after Jehovah had plagued Egypt several times, Pharaoh decided he and his people had suffered enough. He then decided to allow the Israelites to leave Egypt, but Jehovah made him change his mind by hardening his heart, which leads to more pain and suffering for everyone.

Why would Jehovah instigate so much unnecessary fear, pain, and suffering? The following three motives for his behavior come to mind: (1) he is a deranged psychopath who enjoys inflicting fear, pain, and suffering, (2) he is creating an opportunity to demonstrate his destructive power so that he'd be feared by all, or (3) he is preparing the Israelites as a vehicle to subjugate the rest of the peoples in the region. I surmise the answer to the question is all three motives apply.

Section 10
Jehovah Is like a Movie Director

As mentioned earlier, Jehovah previews the future chain of events with Moses in Exodus chapters 3 and 4 before they are acted out. He is like a Hollywood movie director forcing Moses (the main character) and the other Israelites (supporting characters) to follow the script and threatening to replace them if they don't comply.

Section 11
Any Man Can Be Made a God

In Exodus 7:1, Jehovah infers that any man can be made a god when he says to Moses, "I have made thee a god to Pharaoh: and Aaron thy brother shall be thy prophet." Aaron had to speak to the people for Moses because as stated in Exodus 4:10, Moses was "slow of speech, and of a slow tongue." Because of Moses's lack of oratory skill, a chain of command was established where Jehovah spoke to Moses, and Moses then spoke to Aaron, and Aaron finally spoke to the people of Israel. So if Moses was such a lousy speaker and Aaron was such a good one, why didn't Jehovah just bypass Moses and go straight to Aaron? I suggest this was part of Jehovah's plan in setting up a system of control where the hierarchy of priesthood and government mattered more than individual ability. It seemed that Jehovah initiated a type of system that he could manipulate to control the masses of people through a few easily controlled individuals. In other words, Moses was easier to control than Aaron. Recall that Aaron was the maker of the golden calf, which almost led to Jehovah exterminating the Israelites to start over with Moses, replacing Abraham as the seed for his chosen people (Exodus 32:7–10).

Section 12
Three Systems of Control Unified to Work as One

Any prophet who is not controlled by Jehovah is to be killed. This is described in Deuteronomy 18:20, "But the prophet, which shall presume to speak a word in my name, which I have not commanded him to speak, or that shall speak in the name of other gods, even that prophet shall die."

When we examine Jehovah's interaction with humanity, it becomes obvious that his main goal is the complete control of humanity. Jehovah chooses leaders and uses them to set up and maintain three major systems of control. These chosen leaders are referred to as prophets. Some of these leaders were Abraham, Jacob, Moses, Isaiah, Ezekiel, Joseph, Jesus, and later, Muhammad in the Koran.

Let's take a look at the three major systems of control that were installed and utilized by Jehovah for the total control of the minds of the people. These systems are religion, politics, and money. These systems work together as one system, and I refer to them as the Trinity of Control, which parallels the Christian godhead of the Father, Son, and Holy Ghost. And like the Father, Son, and Holy Ghost equals God, religion, politics, and money equals government.

The first system of control is religion. This system of control is set up in the hierarchical pyramid scheme similar to the feudal pyramid of the European Middle Ages. At the top of the pyramid are God, archangels, and angels.

The second level is the prophets such as Moses, Joshua, Ezekiel, and Isaiah.

The third and most significant level is the general populace referred to as sheep, goats, dogs, children, creatures, harvest, etc. This system works as long as the sheep remains obedient to the second-level group on the pyramid (prophets).

This system of religion has, of course, been modified to adapt to today's societies. For example, in the Catholic Church, the pope has replaced the prophet in the second level. The first and third levels of the pyramid have basically remained the same.

The second system of control is politics. This pyramid is also divided into three major sections and is also a top-down control system.

At the top is the primary leader such as president, prime minister, king or queen, sultan, emperor, etc.

The second section consists of an assortment of lesser political officials such as senators, ministers, princes, etc.

At the bottom level are the general populace also referred to as voters, citizens, subjects, peasants, etc., depending on the culture and period in history. This system works as long as the general populace obeys the laws handed down by the first and second levels.

The third and most effective system of control is money. When Jehovah uses and assists the Israelites in subduing and plundering the indigenous peoples of the Middle East, a common theme he emphasizes is, all the wealth, especially gold and silver, is under his control and goes into his treasury. Money is the most effective system of control because it is the fuel that the other two systems of control, religion and politics, need to function, especially in the present form of modern human societies. Political parties, political campaigns, churches, temples, synagogues, and mosques need money to function. Nothing is free; everything costs money. Again, this system works as long as the populace accepts it.

The US monetary system called the Federal Reserve is a prime example of a monetary system of control. The US Federal Reserve system is also organized in a hierarchical pyramid consisting of the Federal Open Market Committee at the top, member banks in the middle, and the US public at the bottom of the pyramid (Buck, 2008). This system works as long as the US public accepts its authority.

Government is the product of the three systems of control. Modern governments have become the most powerful systems of control in human history.

Section 13
Religion + Politics + Money = Government

Note that the word *governmental* is made up of the words *govern* and *mental. Govern* means "control" and *mental* is "of the mind." That is precisely the purpose of today's modern forms of governments around the world—to control the minds of the masses.

The biblical narrative is a historical description of how Jehovah orchestrated the control of the minds of humanity by forcing upon us the aforementioned systems of religion, politics, and money to create the ultimate system of control, which is modern government.

Most adults will agree that in order for people to live together in peace, there needs to be some form of government. I also agree with this idea. However, there is a fine line between a government that helps individuals to grow and realize their potential as sovereign entities, contributing to the welfare of the human community, and a government that oppresses this potential. Today's world governments are constructed and orchestrated to allow the control of the world's human population so that a few individuals may live like the gods of the Bible.

I suggest that the Declaration of Independence and the Constitution of the United States contain good ideas of government. However, good ideas in the hands of greedy, power-hungry individuals are like good seeds planted on barren soil.

Section 14
The Trinity of Control Continues Today

Today, politics, religion, and money continue to be used in controlling the minds of the masses. Together, they comprise the "practical God" of the populace, also known as government.

It is not a coincidence that the president of the United States, when being sworn into office, places his hand on the Bible and swears to continue the system of control forced on humanity, allegedly thousands of years ago, through the concept of a god called Jehovah who is described in that same Bible as "a man of war" (Exodus 15:3).

It is no coincidence that the currency of the Federal Reserve System carries the words In God We Trust as well as the Jewish symbol the Star of David on the back of the one-dollar bill.

Like Jehovah in the Bible, government will do anything to maintain its control, including oppressing and murdering its own people. This is demonstrated in the United States from the American Civil War to the present war on terror, war on crime, war on drugs, war on information, etc. It is no coincidence that Christian governments have played a major role in all major wars in European history including the Crusades, World Wars I and II, and all wars during and since the Cold War.

It is by design that each part of the trinity of control (religion, politics, money) supports one another to work as one system of control. It is by design that Judaism, Christianity, and Islam teach total submission to God and government. It is by design that the US government does not require income tax from religious organizations. It is by design that the government does not allow certain financial institutions to fail as in the "too big to fail" policies demonstrated in the 2008 US financial crisis.

As in the Christian belief in the Holy Trinity of Father, Son, and Holy Ghost, each are part of their godhead called Jehovah. Today's systems of money, politics, and religion are each part of the practical godhead called government, which exists all over the world. The main purpose of this modern form of government is to maintain the status quo, which, in a parasitical fashion, benefits those at the top at the expense of those at the bottom.

A clear symbolic representation of this interrelationship of money, politics, and religion is found on the American one-dollar bill where we find the statement In God We Trust, followed by the Jewish symbol of the Star of David directly above the eagle's head on the right-hand side of the statement. It stands to reason that this god the statement refers to is the Judeo-Christian god Jehovah of the Judeo-Christian Bible.

It should be no surprise that this Star of David is comprised of thirteen five-pointed stars. I suggest that these thirteen stars represent the Christian entities of Jesus and his twelve apostles as well as the thirteen original colonies.

I also suggest that the all-seeing eye inside the capstone of the pyramid on the left-hand side of In God We Trust represents the practical godhead consisting of the holy trinity of money, politics, and religion, which together form government.

All the power attributed to the practical godhead called government could not and would not exist without the cooperation of human individuals. Today's governments are insidiously parasitical in that they draw their power from us in order to exist and to control us for the benefit of the so-called ruling elite. Most of us are not aware of this obvious fact because we are indoctrinated into believing that these parasitical systems of control are benevolent and essential to our existence. The truth of the matter is that these systems of control are the main reason why humanity has been in a perpetual cycle of war, famine, and pestilence (disease) since their inception.

If we follow the biblical narrative, we see Jehovah increasing his effort in forcing these particular systems of control on humanity after he destroyed the metaphoric Tower of Babel described in Genesis 11:1–9 when humanity seemed to be living in peace as one people. Today, the modern system of government continues to be very efficient in keeping humanity divided and at constant war with one another. Millions of people die each year from war and other forms of violence, starvation, and disease as blood sacrifices to keep this global control system going (Lombardo, 2017). It is the modern version of the Old Testament Jehovah's demand for blood sacrifices of both animals and humans.

Section 15
Jehovah Demands Fear and Uses It as
His Primary Control Method

The seminal beginnings of the religions of Judaism, Christianity, and Islam are traced to the prophet Abraham. All three are based on the fear of Jehovah and unquestioned obedience to his commands. Abraham had to prove his fear of Jehovah by following his command to sacrifice his only son Isaac. According to the story, the only reason the killing did not happen is because seconds before he would have murdered his only son, Jehovah's angel arrived and told him he had passed the mind control test as written in Genesis 22:12, "And he said, Lay not thine hand upon the lad, neither do thou any thing unto him: for now I know that thou fearest God, seeing thou hast not withheld thy son, thine only son from me."

It is clear in the above verse that total obedience based on fear is the primary personality trait Jehovah looks for in his chosen leaders. The idea that Jehovah is setting up his kingdom/government on earth fits this personality requirement like a glove if his form of government is totalitarianism.[15]

Throughout the religious literature of Judaism, Christianity, and Islam, we see that fearing and being totally submissive to Jehovah is the most important requirement for being his faithful servant/slave. Abraham was not obedient to Jehovah because he loved him; he was obedient to Jehovah because he feared him. That is not a healthy relationship.

A *proverb* is defined as "a short popular saying that expresses effectively some commonplace truth or useful thought" (Random House, 1992). In Proverbs 1:7, we read, "The fear of the Lord is the beginning of knowledge: but fools despise wisdom and instruction."

A more accurate and truthful saying is "the fear of Jehovah is an obstacle to the truth, hinders the gaining of wisdom, and retards knowledge."

Section 16
People Are Referred to as Farm Animals and Adults as Children

Throughout the Bible, adults are referred to as children and people are generally referred to as farm animals, such as sheep, goats, cattle, dogs, pigs, and creatures. For example, New Testament First John 2:1, "My little children, these things write I unto you, that ye sin not." Referring to grown-ups as little children happens four more times in First John: 2:18, 3:7, 3:18 and 4:4. The children metaphor is also used in Matthew 11:16, "But whereunto shall I liken this generation: It is like unto children sitting in the markets, and calling unto their fellows."

The comparison of people to animals is found in the following verses of the Old and New Testaments. The Old Testament verses are attributed to Jehovah, while the New Testament verses are attributed to his son Jesus:

---

[15] A dictatorial system of government that requires complete subservience

Old Testament

1. "As a shepherd seeketh out his flock in the day that he is among his sheep that are scattered; so will I seek out my sheep" (Ezekiel 34:12).
2. "And as for you, O my flock, thus saith the Lord God; Behold, I judge between cattle and cattle, between the rams and the he goats" (Ezekiel 34:17).

New Testament

1. "And he shall set the sheep on his right hand, but the goats on the left" (Matthew 25:33).
2. "But it is happened unto them according to the true proverb, the dog is turned to its own vomit again, and the sow that was washed to her wallowing in the mire" (Second Peter 2:22)
3. "Give not that which is holy unto the dogs, neither cast ye your pearls before swine" (Matthew 7:6).
4. "Go ye into all the world, and preach the gospel to every creature" (Mark 16:15).

Taking into account the obvious, comparing of people to farm animals and Jehovah's demand for total submission, Jesus in the following verse is easily interpreted as saying, "If these animals cannot be completely mind controlled, they need to be destroyed!"

"He that believeth and is baptized shall be saved; but he that believeth not shall be damned" (Mark 16:16).

In the book of Matthew, Jesus compares people to sheep and as a farm product that needs to be harvested as written in Matthew 9:36–38:

> But when he saw the multitudes, he was moved with compassion on them, because they fainted, and were scattered abroad, as sheep having no shepherd. Then saith he unto his disciples, The harvest truly is plenteous,

but the labourers are few; Pray ye therefore the Lord of
the harvest, that he will send forth labourers into his
harvest.

Who are the laborers, and what is the harvest in the above metaphoric
narrative? I suggest the laborers and the harvest are us. Jesus is the farmer,
and Jehovah is the owner of the farm. Everyone under the control of
the farm/government is simply a commodity for consumption by the
farmer Jesus, his father Jehovah, and the other gods.

The only way out of this control system is individual rebellion from
within—a mental and spiritual rebellion. Your rebellion will not succeed
if you have to depend on a leader other than yourself. You need to lead
yourself in order to obtain true freedom based on love and truth. The
love of the truth will help you set yourself free.

Section 17
Jehovah Uses Extreme Violence as Punishment
for Not Following His Commandments

The Israelites are severely punished for not fearing Jehovah. Minor,
petty crimes such as gathering sticks on the Sabbath are punished by
stoning to death. For breaking the Sabbath and worshipping other gods,
Jehovah punishes the Israelites by inflicting them with disease, famine,
wars, genocide, and having them eat the flesh of their own children.

In Exodus 15:26, Jehovah issues a subtle threat of punishment by
disease if the Israelites don't follow his rules and commands, "If thou
wilt diligently hearken to the voice of the Lord thy God, and wilt do
that which is right in his sight, and wilt give ear to his commandments,
and keep all his statutes, I will put none of these diseases upon thee,
which I have brought upon the Egyptians: for I am the Lord that healeth
thee."

To paraphrase, Jehovah is saying, "I will not punish you with diseases
like I did the Egyptians as long as you follow my exact commands, do
what I say is right and ignore your natural sense of right and wrong,

and follow all the rituals and laws I have forced on you; because I am the one that heals you from the diseases I inflict on you."

There is an incident in Exodus chapter 32 where Jehovah becomes angry because the Israelites are worshipping a golden calf. He decides to kill them all and regenerate the tribe through Moses, but Moses convinces him to change his mind.

In the above incident, Moses talks Jehovah out of killing all the Israelites by reminding him of the promise he had made to Abraham. He also says that the Egyptians will lose respect for him and will say that he took the Israelites out of Egypt just to kill them in the desert. This incident further demonstrates that Jehovah is just a man who easily loses his temper and makes irrational decisions based on his anger. In this case, Moses talks him out of making a hasty decision that he may have later regretted. Jehovah feeds his thirst for blood and violence anyway by having three thousand men killed for worshipping the golden calf as written in Exodus 32:27–28:

> Go in and out from gate to gate throughout the camp, and slay every man his brother, and every man his companion, and every man his neighbor. And the children of Levi did according to the word of Moses: and there fell of the people that day about three thousand men.

Jehovah then later plagues them for the same crime in Exodus 32:35, "And the Lord plagued the people, because they made the calf, which Aaron made."

In Exodus 35:2, Moses tells the Israelites that one of Jehovah's commandments is that they are to work six days a week and rest on the seventh day. The punishment for breaking this commandment is death. An example of this is found in Numbers 15:32–36 where a man was arrested for gathering sticks while in the wilderness, and as punishment, Jehovah orders the congregation to stone him to death. Death is also the punishment for cursing and blasphemy (Leviticus 24:14, 16).

The third book of Moses called Leviticus is full of rituals and commandments from Jehovah that the Israelites are commanded to follow. If they do not follow all his commandments including animal sacrifice and blood rituals to his specific instructions, he threatens them with a barrage of punishments, which includes making them eat the flesh of their sons and daughters. Leviticus 26:29, "And ye shall eat the flesh of your sons, and the flesh of your daughters shall ye eat."

The following biblical account happened during a famine Jehovah has inflicted on the people for breaking one or more of his commandments. In the narrative, a woman is upset because she has boiled and shared her son's flesh with another woman, but the other woman is not keeping her promise to do the same with her own son as written in Second Kings 6:28–29:

> And the king said unto her, What aileth thee? And she answered, This woman said unto me, Give thy son, that we may eat him today, and we will eat my son tomorrow. So we boiled my son, and did eat him: and I said unto her the next day, Give thy son, that we may eat him: and she hath hid her son.

Such is the way Jehovah manifests his alleged love for his chosen people.

In Numbers chapter 16, Jehovah killed 250 men with fire for speaking out against Moses and Aaron and for inappropriately offering incense to him. Apparently, offering incense to Jehovah was considered a crime if you were not a priest descended from Aaron, the same Aaron that made the golden calf that led to Jehovah killing more than 3,000 Israelis. Jehovah then killed 14,700 more Israelis for complaining about his killing the 250 that had spoken out against Moses and Aaron. That is a total of 17,950 people killed for the initial crime of complaining.

In Numbers 21:5–6, Jehovah killed many more Israelites for speaking out against him and Moses.

In Numbers 25:1–9, Jehovah had many Israelites beheaded then killed 24,000 more with a plague for worshipping other gods. As written in Numbers 25:4, "And the Lord said unto Moses take all the heads of the people, and hang them up before the Lord against the sun, that the fierce anger of the Lord may be turned away from Israel," and in Numbers 25:9, "And those that died in the plague were twenty and four thousand."

Again, Jehovah's objective is total control through fear. He not only wanted the people of that time to fear him but their descendants as well.

Deuteronomy 4:10. "Gather me the people together, and I will make them hear my words, that they may learn to fear me all the days that they shall live upon the earth and that they may teach their children."

Deuteronomy 6:2. "Fear the Lord thy God, to keep all his statutes and his commandments, which I command thee, thou, and thy son, and thy son's son."

Deuteronomy 6:13. "Thou shalt fear the Lord thy God, and serve him, and shalt swear by his name."

Jehovah's behavior is analogous to the cruel slave master who demands his slaves to fear him because he believes that is the best way to control them. The indigenous people who are aware of the destructive power of Jehovah are so terrified they faint with fear when the Israelites arrive in their area, as described in Joshua 2:24.

Another example of maniacal punishment for not fearing this self-proclaimed god is given in Second Kings 17:25 where Jehovah sets lions loose on people for not fearing him. Second Kings 17:34–36 are more reminders that he is the only god they should fear and perform blood sacrifices to, and once again, reminds them that he is the one who brought them out of Egypt. These verses are also a reminder that there are other gods in the Bible that Jehovah is competing against for control of the minds of the people.

In the book of Exodus, after Jehovah killed all the Egyptians that were pursuing the Israelites, it becomes clear that fear is the main controlling factor that he has over them as written in Exodus 14:31, "And Israel saw that great work which the Lord did upon the Egyptians: and the people feared the Lord, and believed the Lord, and his servant Moses."

Section 18
Dashing Children to Pieces in Front of Their Parents and the Raping of Wives and Mothers Used as Punishment

The book of Isaiah is full of more cruelness, more demands for total submission, and more threats of total destruction for noncompliance. Here is an example from Isaiah 13:15–16 concerning punishment for noncompliance, "Everyone that is found shall be thrust through; and every one that is joined unto them shall fall by the sword. Their children also shall be dashed to pieces before their eyes; their house shall be spoiled, and their wives ravished."

In Isaiah 1:15, Jehovah admonishes the Israelites, telling them that their hands are full of blood. This admonishment against the Israelites is coming from a man of war who orders ripping out the fetuses of pregnant women, dashing infants against stone, the raping of wives and mothers, forcing parents to eat their own children, and the stoning to death of anyone caught gathering sticks on the Sabbath.

The worshippers of this murdering psychopath Jehovah expect you and me to believe that he is a just and loving god. This reminds me of the battered wife syndrome. When the wife who is repeatedly brutally beaten by her husband tries to protect him each time while insisting that he loves her and proclaiming that he is not really a bad guy because his abuse is motivated by his love for her.

CHAPTER 5

JEHOVAH PROMOTES WAR AND PROVIDES ADVANCED MILITARY TECHNOLOGY

Section 1
Jehovah Is a Man of War Who Provides
Moses with Advanced Weaponry

Modern education systems today have indoctrinated us into believing that we are the most advanced society in the history of the world. However, there are many examples of evidence that contradict this dogmatic view of history, too many to mention in this book. An example of this evidence is a human skull estimated to be approximately 125,000 to 300,000 years old with a bullet hole (Holloway, 2014). A similar bullet hole was found in the skull of an auroch, an extinct wild cattle that lived between 2 million and 4,000 years ago (ibid). This is a minute example of archeological evidence that advanced technology existed millions of years before the time period we are indoctrinated into believing through our government controlled education systems.

It is reasonable to suggest that Jehovah and other gods of the Bible possessed very advanced technologies that they used to promote themselves as gods. The biblical narrative is full of inferences to these technologies. It appears that Jehovah made some of these advanced technologies available to some of his chosen prophets such as Moses and Joshua for the process of subjugating the surrounding groups of indigenous peoples.

In Numbers 1:3, Jehovah commands Moses to form a military draft. An example of Jehovah the man of war providing Moses and the Israelites with superior military technology is described in Exodus 17:9–12. Moses directs Joshua to choose some men to fight against Amalek. He tells him he will be standing on top a hill with the "rod of God" in his hand. The inference is that this "rod of God" will guarantee victory.

This is the way the ensuing battle was described: Moses along with Aaron and Hur is on top of the hill, using the "rod of God" against the opposing army. They were winning as long as Moses kept the rod of God engaged on the enemy but began losing whenever Moses's arm got tired and let the weapon down. Aaron and Hur assisted Moses in propping the weapon provided by Jehovah on a rock and helped him hold it steady as he fired it. It stands to reason that the "rod of God" is clearly a type of advanced weapon provided to Moses by Jehovah.

Section 2
Jehovah Also Provides Joshua with Superior Weaponry and Military Strategy

In Joshua chapter 8, Jehovah commanded Joshua to go to the city of Ai and do what they had recently done to the city of Jericho. They had recently annihilated that city and taken all its gold and silver and killed all the men, women, children, and animals.

As he had provided Moses with the "rod of God," Jehovah also provided Joshua with an advanced weapon referred to as a spear and instructed him to set up an ambush. As they attacked the city of Ai, he told Joshua to stretch the weapon at the city until everyone in the city is dead as written in Joshua 8:18–19 and 25–26:

> And the Lord said unto Joshua, Stretch out the
> spear that is in thy hand toward Ai; for I will give it

unto thy hand. And Joshua stretched out the spear that he had in his hand toward the city. And the ambush arose quickly out of their place, and they ran as he had stretched out his hand: and they entered into the city, and took it, and hasted and set the city on fire.

And so it was, that all that fell that day, both of men and women, were twelve thousand, even all the men of Ai. For Joshua drew not his hand back, wherewith he stretched out the spear until he had utterly destroyed all the inhabitants of Ai.

The weapon provided to Joshua appeared to have been lighter and easier to use because he did not need assistance in firing it as had Moses. The destruction and plunder of Ai is another example of how Jehovah assisted the Israelites by providing them with military strategy and advanced weaponry. It is reasonable to interpret Joshua's spear, which he stretches toward the city of Ai, as an advanced weapon provided by Jehovah that he aims and fires as directed by Jehovah. Joshua's army attacked after he began firing the weapon at the city. And as verse 26 described, he did not stop firing the weapon until all the inhabitants of the city of Ai were killed.

Section 3
Jehovah Travels in Advanced Military Aircraft Directly Assisting The Israelites in Their Wars of Aggression Against the Indigenous Peoples of the Middle East

"And the Lord went before them by day in a pillar of a cloud, to lead them thy way; and by night in a pillar of fire, to give them light; to go by day and night" (Exodus 13:21). Note that the Lord is in the pillar of a cloud and in the pillar of fire. It stands to reason that the pillar of a cloud and pillar of fire are metaphors for aircraft that the Lord is traveling in. In Exodus 14:24–25, we see another example of advanced technology and Jehovah fighting directly for Israel against the Egyptians, "And it came to pass, that in the morning watch the Lord looked unto the host of the Egyptians through the pillar of fire and of the cloud, and troubled the host of the Egyptians, And took off their chariot wheels, that they drave them heavily; so that the Egyptians said, Let us flee from the face of Israel; for the Lord fighteth for them against the Egyptians."

Note that the Lord is traveling in the sky in a pillar of a cloud and in a pillar of fire, which may very well be a type of holographic camouflage. He looks down upon the Egyptians and Israelites from inside of these aircraft. These aircraft are sometimes referred to as chariots of fire in other biblical passages (2 Kings 6:17; Isaiah 66:15; Joel 2:5). Today these same vehicles might be described as UFOs. Note that in verse 25, the Egyptians were terrified that Jehovah is now directly assisting the Israelites.

Section 4
Jehovah Attacks from the Sky in His Military Aircraft, and the Israelites Kill Those Who Remain Alive

In Joshua 10:11, we read about an aerial attack by Jehovah against the city of Azekah, where he is providing air support for the Israelis as they attack the city. It is reasonable to interpret the biblical description of the Lord casting down hailstones and great stones from heaven to be military aircraft firing bullets and dropping bombs on the city. I believe the narrator is describing a military aerial assault on the city of Azekah, and not having the technical terminology available, he uses figurative language to describe what he is witnessing.

Section 5
Did Jehovah Use Nuclear Weapons to Destroy Sodom and Gomorrah?

In Genesis chapter 19, Jehovah and two angels used a weapon that completely destroyed the cities of Sodom and Gomorrah and every living thing in the cities, including everything that grows on the ground. Before he destroyed Sodom, he took Abraham's nephew Lot and his wife and two daughters outside the city and told them to get off the flat plain and go into the mountains. He told Lot he would not destroy the city until he and his family were safe in the mountains (Genesis 19:16–22). For some reason, Lot's wife lagged behind, perhaps she wanted to witness the destruction close-up. It appeared that she ended up being vaporized by the weapon used to destroy the city as written in Genesis 19:1, 19:13, and 19:24–28:

> And there came two angels to Sodom at even.[16]
>
> For we will destroy this place . . . the Lord has sent us to destroy it.
>
> Then the Lord rained upon Sodom and upon Gomorrah brimstone and fire from the Lord out of heaven; And he overthrew those cities, and all the plain, and all the inhabitants of the cities, and that which grew upon the ground. But his wife looked back from behind him, and she became a pillar of salt, And Abraham gat up early in the morning to the place where he stood before the Lord: And he looked toward Sodom and Gomorrah, and toward all the land of the plain, and beheld, and, lo, the smoke of the country went up as the smoke of a furnace.

Paraphrasing the above account, Jehovah and his companions flew over Sodom and Gomorrah in some type of aircraft and dropped a nuclear bomb on each of those cities. The bombs annihilated the cities, killing every living thing including the vegetation. Lot's wife, out of curiosity, stayed behind, got too close to the explosion, and was vaporized. Abraham got up early in the morning and went to the location where he had fed Jehovah and his two companions the previous day on their way to Sodom and Gomorrah. From that location, Abraham

---

[16]   Archaic form of *evening*

looked toward Sodom and Gomorrah and observed the funnel-like smoke from the smoldering remains rising into the sky.

This is reminiscent of the description of the cities of Hiroshima and Nagasaki after they, too, were annihilated during World War II.

Two other cities besides Sodom and Gomorrah were destroyed by what appears to also be nuclear weapons. These two cities are mentioned later in Deuteronomy where the aftermath of their destruction is described along with Sodom and Gomorrah. The two cities are called Admah and Zeboim. The following verses describe some of the immediate effects of the destruction and what people from a generation (twenty-five years) after the destruction would see. What is described also resembles the aftermath of a nuclear explosion. The narrator describes the land as "brimstone, salt, and burning," where nothing can be grown, not even grass because the soil is so burnt. This is described in Deuteronomy 29:22–24.

Section 6
Militarily Inferior People Are Perceived as Prey by Jehovah and the Israelites

The following are two examples of predatory scripture describing how Jehovah and the Israelites perceive militarily inferior peoples as prey:

1. "Behold, the people shall rise up as a great lion, and lift up himself as a young lion: he shall not lie down until he eat of the prey, and drink the blood of the slain" (Numbers 23:24).

Israel, of course, is the great young lion that eats and drinks the blood of the indigenous peoples.

2. "Take the sum of the prey that was taken, both of man and beast . . . And divide the prey into two parts" (Numbers 31:26–27).

Section 7
Surrender or Be Killed

In the fifth book of Moses called Deuteronomy, Jehovah commands the Israeli army to go and offer peace to the cities. If they accept the terms for peace, they are forced to work for the Israelites and pay tributaries[17]. However, if they refuse the conditions of the peace offering and defend themselves, Jehovah steps in with superior military technology to make sure they are defeated. As punishment for defending themselves, all the males are killed and all the women, children, cattle, and everything of material value are captured for consumption by the Israelis. For certain cities, Jehovah commands that everything that breathes be killed. That includes women, infant children, cattle, and pets. This is written in Deuteronomy 20:10–17.

These acts of genocide are committed to exterminate the inhabitants in order for the Israelites to take possession of the land. Three thousand years later, the Christian countries of Spain and England do the same to the indigenous peoples of North and South America.

Section 8
Despite His Advanced Weaponry, Jehovah Finally Suffers Defeat

In Joshua 10:42, we read, "And all these kings and their land did Joshua take at one time, because the Lord God of Israel fought for Israel." Jehovah was personally participating in Joshua's conquest of all the kingdoms he directed him to invade. It was no contest on the battlefield for Joshua because Jehovah was supporting him with advanced military technology as they easily overwhelmed the enemy.

In the book of Judges, the killing and the pillaging continue with the Lord leading the way with advanced weaponry. However, he finally suffered a defeat in the Gaza area as written in Judges 1:18–19:

---

[17]   Payments such as taxes or other items of value

> Also Judah took Gaza with the coast thereof, and
> Askelon with the coast thereof, and Ekron with the
> coast thereof. And the Lord was with Judah; and he
> drave out the inhabitants of the mountain; but could
> not drive out the inhabitants of the valley, because they
> had chariots of iron.

Wow! The alleged Almighty God could not defeat an army that uses chariots of iron. Why? The answer is very simple. He is just another man who can be defeated as seen in Genesis 32:24–30 where Jacob defeated him in a wrestling match. He is just a man of war as stated in Exodus 15:3. The only thing that makes him a god is his access to superior technology. Anyone can be a god or goddess if they have superior technology at their disposal as long as the people they live among remain with extremely inferior technology.

All of a sudden, Jehovah and the Israelites cannot defeat the targeted prey "because they had chariots of iron." What may these "chariots of iron" be? I don't think they were the stereotypical chariots pulled by horses that we are shown in history books and movies because the military weaponry provided by Jehovah described in the biblical scriptures would easily have defeated those.

It stands to reason that a rival god provided the targeted prey of the Israelites with advanced military technology as Jehovah was providing the Israelites. The targeted prey was now able to successfully defend themselves against Jehovah and the Israelites.

Section 9
Other Indigenous Peoples Who Jehovah Could Not Completely Defeat

There are other indigenous peoples mentioned who could not be driven out or defeated by Jehovah and the Israelites. The following are examples of some of those groups of people:

1. "And the children of Benjamin did not drive out the Jebusites that inhabited Jerusalem; but the Jebusites dwell with the children of Benjamin in Jerusalem unto this day" (Judges 1:21). Note that the Palestinians today are said to be the descendants of the Canaanite Jebusites (Wenkel, 2007).
2. "Neither did Manasseh drive out the inhabitants of Bethshean and her towns, nor Taanach and her towns, nor the inhabitants of Dor and her towns, nor the inhabitants of Ibleam and her towns, nor the inhabitants of Megiddo and her towns: but the Canaanites would dwell in that land" (Judges 1:27).
3. "Neither did Ephraim drive out the Canaanites that dwelt in Gezer; but the Canaanites dwelt in Gezer among them" (Judges 1:29).

The main idea here is that Jehovah, the god of Israel, finally started losing some battles because another god or gods began supplying other peoples with advanced military technology to keep Jehovah and the Israelites from taking complete control of the entire contested area. The other gods proved that Jehovah could be defeated in war, thus removing his exaggerated persona of invincibility.

Section 10
The Fight for Control of the Middle East Continues Today with the United States Replacing Jehovah in Supplying the Region with Military Technology

The contest for control of the Middle East continues today. The Jewish state of Israel today has been in conflict with most of its neighbors since its creation in 1948. Modern Israel was created after World War II. The United Kingdom and the United States were the two most influential governments in creating Israel. They have and continue to supply it with state-of-the-art military technology. Modern Israel was created by violently removing the Palestinian people from land they had been living on for over a thousand years.

The United States is analogous to the biblical Old Testament god Jehovah in its favorable treatment of the modern state of Israel. Besides providing it with superior military technology since its creation, the US also gives Israel billions of dollars annually in financial support. All this wealth is given to Israel at the expense of the American taxpayers.

I believe that Jehovah, the man of war, is still alive today in the spiritual and mental domains of today's modern governments and still exerting his influence, primarily through influential governments such as the United States, Russia, China, Britain, France, Germany, Israel, Saudi Arabia, et al. He is like a spiritual virus.

Section 11
The Worship of Jehovah Promotes the Idea That Brutal, Murderous, Cowardly Behavior Is Acceptable

The description of the Old Testament Jehovah and Israelites' invasion of the Middle East is imitated by every Christian empire on practically every continent on earth in their never-ending quest for material wealth.

The fate of the Old Testament indigenous tribes of the Hittites, Amorites, Canaanites, Perizzites, Hivites, and Jebusites parallel the fate of the Native American tribes such as the Taino, Mexica, Inca, Cree, Delaware, Shawnee, Montagnais, Huron, Miami, Cherokee, Iroquois, Sioux, Mohawk, Mohican, Mississippian, Nez Perce, Hohokam, Comanche, Kiowa, Apache, Navajo, Hopi, et al.

The Judeo-Christian European governments including the United States have taken up the mantle of Old Testament Israel in fulfilling the following script or scripture, "Thus shalt thou do unto all the cities which are very far off from thee, which are not of the cities of these nations" (Deuteronomy 20:17). It seems that the man of war already had plans of using his followers to take control of the rest of the world. Millions of indigenous peoples on every continent have suffered similar military invasions at the hands of the Judeo-Christian Europeans that the indigenous peoples of the Old Testament suffered at the hands of the Israelites and their biblical man of war, Jehovah.

The Christian nations of Western, Northern, Central, and Southern Europe went into Africa and the Americas like a pack of marauding beasts devouring all militarily inferior indigenous cultures in their path. The hunger that motivates them to such behavior is the greed for wealth and power. It is basically the same insane hunger as that of Jehovah and the Israelites of the Old Testament.

It is not coincidental that the two most powerful imperial empires that invaded North and South America are also Judeo-Christian. Christianity is practically a branch of Judaism. The Judeo-Christian Bible is called that because it is a combination of the Jewish and Christian bibles. Recall that Jesus was a Jew, and so were the twelve apostles.

The Judeo-Christian Spanish and British empires were the most successful in these wars of pillage and plunder, paralleling the Israelites of the Old Testament. Today, it is the United States of America carrying the mantle of Jehovah and the Old Testament warmongering Israelites. Like the Israelites, they would not have had the success they did without superior weaponry.

Section 12
Jehovah's Rocket Technology

More advanced technology resembling a type of flying vehicle that used powerful rocket engines is described in Exodus 19:16 and 19:18, "And it came to pass on the third day in the morning, that there were thunders and lightnings, and a thick cloud upon the mount, and the voice of the trumpet exceeding loud; so that all the people that was in the camp trembled." "And mount Sinai was altogether on a smoke, because the Lord descended upon it in fire; and the smoke thereof ascended as the smoke of a furnace and the whole mount quaked greatly."

This sounds like the description of a huge rocket-powered craft landing on Mount Sinai. The narrator uses figurative language to describe the fire and noise coming from the rocket's exhaust system, which is described as thunder and lightning that makes the mountain quake. It is kicking up huge clouds of dust and smoke as it lands on the mountain.

Section 13
The Ark of the Covenant Is a Communication Device and a Weapon That Caused Tumors in the Genitals

Two more examples of advanced technology are found in Numbers 7:89–8:1 and First Samuel 5:8–12. In the first example, after a blood sacrifice, the Lord spoke with Moses using the ark of testimony, also called the ark of the covenant and the ark of God. This is a device made of gold and silver that was created using specific directions from Jehovah and is used as a communication device and as a weapon as written in Numbers 7:89 and 8:1:

> And when Moses was gone into the tabernacle of the congregation to speak with him, then he heard the voice of one speaking unto him from off the mercy seat that was upon the ark of testimony, from between the two cherubims: and he spake unto him.
> And the Lord spake unto Moses.

In the above verses, Moses went into a tentlike structure referred to as a tabernacle, where the ark of the covenant was located for the purpose of speaking with God. He heard God's voice coming from a specific part of the ark of the covenant and proceeded to speak with him.

In the following verses, the Philistines took the ark of the covenant into their city. They apparently had no control over the device because Jehovah used it to destroy their city and cause tumors in the private parts of the inhabitants. They then moved it to a different city where the same thing happened as written in First Samuel 5:9–10:

And it was so, that, after they had carried it about, the hand of the Lord was against the city with a very great destruction: and he smote the men of the city, both small and great, and they had emerods[18] in their secret parts . . . The Ekronites cried out, saying, They have brought about the ark of the God of Israel to us, to slay us and our people.

For those that are not aware, certain types of radiation such as from nuclear weapons are said to cause cancerous tumors. In the above scripture, we can see that the city inhabitants that the ark of the covenant was used against were inflicted with "emerods," or tumors.

Section 14
Jehovah Kills 50,070 Men Just for Looking into the Ark of the Covenant

In Samuel 6:19, Jehovah killed 50,070 men just for looking into the ark of the covenant, "And he smote the men of Bethshemesh, because they had looked into the ark of the Lord, even he smote of the people fifty thousand and threescore and ten men."

Why would Jehovah kill 50,070 men just for looking into the ark of the covenant? By now, it should be obvious to the reader that human life to Jehovah means very little; killing tens of thousands at a time is trivial to him.

Section 15
Jehovah Uses Cloaking and Holographic Technology

In Exodus 14:19–20, we see what seems to be a type of holographic cloaking device being used by Jehovah in the desert to protect the fleeing Israelites from the pursuing Egyptians:

---

[18] Tumors

> And the angel of God, which went before the camp of
> Israel, removed and went behind them; and the pillar of
> the cloud went from before their face, and stood behind
> them. And it came between the camp of the Egyptians
> and the camp of Israel; and it was a cloud and darkness
> to them, but it gave light by night to these: so that the
> one came not near the other all the night.

To paraphrase, though they were in close proximity to each other, the separate camps of the Egyptians and Israelites were not aware of each other because of "the angel of God" (technologically advanced aircraft) that placed itself in between the two camps. To the Egyptians, it appeared as a dark cloud, while at the same time, to the Israelites viewing the same object from the opposite side, it appeared as a light. The practical interpretation of the above scripture is that the holographic cloaking technology made the physical setting appear as a cloud and darkness to the Egyptians, but to the Israelites, it provided light so they could keep moving to escape from the Egyptians.

There is an account in First Kings where the narrator describes an event where the prophet Elijah has an experience that may also be describing a cloaking technology as written in First Kings 19:11–13:

> And he said, Go forth, and stand upon the mount
> before the Lord. And, behold, the Lord passed by, and
> a great and strong wind rent the mountains, and brake
> in pieces the rocks before the Lord; but the Lord was
> not in the wind: and after the wind an earthquake;
> but the Lord was not in the earthquake: And after the
> earthquake a fire; but the Lord was not in the fire: and
> after the fire a still small voice. And it was so, when
> Elijah heard it, that he wrapped his face in his mantle,
> and went out, and stood in the entering in of the cave.
> And, behold, there came a voice unto him, and said,
> What doest thou here, Elijah?

In the above account, the prophet Elijah observed what is described as a strong wind, followed by an earthquake that is tearing the mountain, breaking rocks, causing a fire, and shaking the earth, but he could not see what was causing it. He said that it was the Lord causing all the commotion but also said that the Lord was not visible. Elijah then took shelter in a cave until he heard a "still, small voice," which caused him to wrap his mantle around his face and stand at the cave entrance. He then heard a voice asking him what he was doing there.

It seemed that the narrator was describing Elijah experiencing the landing of a large rocket-powered aircraft similar to the one that had landed on Mount Sinai described in Exodus 19:17–19. The craft is using cloaking technology so as not to be seen, but the effects of the landing are very apparent. Elijah apparently took cover in a cave as the powerful craft was landing.

Again, the person in the story who recounted this event could only describe it in terms he was familiar with. It is not difficult to imagine describing the effects of a large rocket ship that is landing in close proximity to you as "a strong wind followed by an earthquake." It is tearing the mountain, breaking rocks, causing a fire, and shaking the earth.

Section 16
Elijah's Mantle Is Used to Part the River Jordan

What was prophet Elijah's mantle[19] made of that allowed him to use it to part the waters of the River Jordan? He used it to part the waters so he and his apprentice Elisha could walk across. The account was described in Second Kings 2:7–8. I thinkElijah's mantle was another form of advanced technology that Jehovah and the other gods were using.

---

[19] A long loose cape-like garment

Section 17
Elijah Calls for Military Assistance from
the Sky That Kills Fifty Soldiers

Some prophets such as Elijah seem to have direct military authority to order attacks on specific targets. For example, in one account, Elijah called down what was described as "fire from heaven" that killed fifty soldiers who were trying to apprehend him. In the account, Elijah was conversing with the captain of fifty soldiers as written in Second Kings 1:12, "And Elijah answered and said unto them, If I be a man of God, let fire come down from heaven, and consume thee and thy fifty. And the fire of God came down from heaven, and consumed him and his fifty."

I believe that in the above account, there was at least one aircraft hovering over the scene and that Elijah was in communication with the occupants of that craft. At his request or command, the aircraft fired on the fifty soldiers, obliterating them.

Fast-forward to July 12, 2007, Baghdad, Iraq, after the US and British invasion. In this account, a group of men were gathered on a street corner. The men were unaware they were being observed and videotaped through the gunsight camera of a high-flying US helicopter until the pilot opened fire on them (Wikileaks, 2019). The group of Iraqi men was obliterated by the machine-gun fire, as were the captain and his fifty soldiers in the Elijah account.

Though both events are separated by at least three thousand years, the similarities between them are that they both occurred in the same geographic region and that both groups of men were not even aware they were being observed by hovering military aircraft until they were fired upon.

Section 18
Elijah Is Taken Up in an Aircraft

The prophet Elijah was eventually taken away in a flying craft as written in Second Kings 2:11, "And it came to pass, as they still went on, and talked, that, behold, there appeared a chariot of fire, and horses of fire, and parted them both asunder, and Elijah went up by a whirlwind into heaven."

Let's take a closer look at what the narrator is describing in the above verse. This event is one in a chain of events described in Second Kings chapters 1 and 2 concerning the prophet Elijah and his apprentice Elisha as they traveled through the region known today as the Middle East. Elijah was working directly for Jehovah and interacting on his behalf with kings and other members of the ruling class of that time.

As they were walking and talking, an object suddenly appeared in the sky that was described as "chariot of fire and horses of fire." It stands to reason that this object that appeared was a vehicle that could be used for transportation, as chariots were used for transportation. Horses were used to pull chariots, so it stands to reason that the "horses of fire" were part of the "chariot of fire." This vehicle separated Elijah from Elisha and took him up into the sky. According to the Bible narrative, he was not seen again until approximately nine hundred years later as described in Matthew 17:3 during the time of the New Testament Jesus.

This vehicle that was described as a chariot and horses of fire could be a description of a helicopter with flashing red, green, orange, and yellow lights. It was described as "a chariot and horses of fire" because it was used to transport Elijah and the narrator was attempting to describe technology that he had no technical words for, so he used metaphoric language instead. The helicopter blades were churning the air and kicking up dust similar to a whirlwind or powerful dust devil. It hovered above Elijah as it took him on board and then flew away.

There is a helicopter carved on an Egyptian temple constructed during the reign of the pharaoh Seti that looks like a modern helicopter. This temple is said to have been built approximately 430 years before the above event took place. There is, of course, disagreement among researchers concerning the validity of the Seti helicopter. Some say it is an anomaly caused by overlapping carvings on the same surface; some disagree (Wikipedia, 20019).

Section 19
Jehovah Orders a Scorched-Earth Policy against the Moabites

The following quote from Second Kings 3:19 describes Jehovah ordering the Israelites to carry out a war strategy resembling a scorched-earth policy on a people called the Moabites: "And ye shall smite every fenced city, and every choice city, and shall fell every good tree, and stop all wells of water, and mar every good piece of land with stones." During the US Civil War, General Sherman carried out a similar war strategy to help defeat the Confederacy. It is known as Sherman's March to the Sea and as Sherman's March through Georgia.

Section 20
Jehovah Intervenes with Superior Military
Technology to Save Maccabeus

Another example of Jehovah intervening on behalf of the Israelites and using superior military technology during battle is described in Second Maccabees 10:29–31:

> But when the battle waxed strong, there appeared unto the enemies from heaven five comely men upon horses, with bridles of gold, and two of them led the Jews. And took Maccabeus betwixt them, and covered him on every side weapons, and kept him safe, but shot arrows and lightnings against the enemies: so that they being confounded with blindness, and full of trouble, they were killed. And there were slain of footmen twenty thousand and five hundred, and six hundred horsemen.

Paraphrasing the above scripture, in the middle of an intense battle, there appeared five attractive men in the sky in some type of aircraft, and with advanced weapons, surrounded Maccabeus, protecting him from all sides while killing 25,500 foot soldiers and 600 cavalry of the opposing army.

This direct intervention by Jehovah using his advanced military technology allowed Maccabeus to win the battle. The narrator uses "arrows and lightnings" as metaphors to describe his observation of advanced weaponry. Again, one must reason that the narrator did not have the technical terminology to use in describing the observed weaponry other than in the metaphoric language he was familiar with. It is obvious that the weapons provided and used by Jehovah are not the ordinary weapons that today's government education systems teaches existed at that time.

Section 21
Advanced Technology Is Used to Promote Christianity

The use of superior technology was used militarily and also in other ways to promote the spread of Christianity. The story of the conversion of Saul of Tarsus to Christianity infers the use of advanced technology in a nonlethal way. The account is found in Acts 9:3–9. It describes Saul being blinded by a light in the sky. He hears a voice that claims to be Jesus who had recently been killed as a blood sacrifice. Saul's companions apparently did not see the light that blinded Saul, but they did hear a voice. Saul did not eat nor drink for three days at which time he regained his sight. After this incident, he quit persecuting the Christians and played a significant role in the spread of Christianity as the apostle Paul.

There was an incident in Luke 9:51–56 where Jesus was not received well in a certain village. It seemed that the village inhabitants were not giving Jesus the respect that his disciples James and John felt he should have received. They then asked Jesus if he wanted them to call down fire from heaven to consume the villagers. This was what Elijah the prophet had done approximately nine hundred years before in the Old Testament account found in First Kings 18:36–40. The idea that Elijah of the Old Testament and James and John of the New Testament could call down fire from heaven to kill people at their discretion implied that these characters were in regular contact with entities that provided access to advanced military technology.

Section 22
The Plunder of Jericho Has Been Sugarcoated

When I was an eight-year-old child being indoctrinated into the Catholic Christian religion, we were told the story of Jericho and how Joshua blew a ram's horn and the Israelites shouted to make the walls that surrounded the city fall down. The impression of the story is that it was a triumphant, joyous event that demonstrated the love Jehovah had for the Jews and the Christians.

I do not think that most of us today have actually read the complete story in the Bible about Joshua and Jericho. Most of us are unaware that Jehovah ordered all the silver and gold and other precious metals of the city to be put in his treasury, all the men women and children murdered, and all the farm animals killed. Everyone and everything in the city is killed except for a prostitute and her family who helped the Israelites by spying on the city before Jehovah and the Israelites destroyed it. The account is described in Joshua 6:19–24. Again, more gold and silver for the man of war's treasury gained by murdering and plundering.

A similar brutal massacre is also described in Second Maccabees 12:15–16 where Judas and the Israelites, aided by Jehovah, destroyed and plundered the city of Caspis, which, like Jericho, was also surrounded by very strong walls: "Wherefore Judas with his company, calling upon the great Lord of the world, . . . gave a fierce assault against the walls. And took the city by the will of God and made unspeakable slaughters, insomuch that a lake two furlongs[20] broad near adjoining thereunto, being filled full, was seen running with blood."

It stands to reason that if the walls of Jericho crumbled simply by blowing on rams' horns and the shouting of thousands of people,

---

[20]   440 yards

then all the football stadiums around the world today should have crumbled a long time ago. According to archeologists, the walls of Jericho were approximately six feet thick (The Walls of Jericho, 2019). Obviously, something else made the walls crumble. It stands to reason that Jehovah's advanced military technology was utilized in destroying the walls of Jericho and Caspis.

Another hint that Jehovah was utilizing advanced weaponry in helping the Israelites conquer the peoples around them is seen in Leviticus 26:8, "And five of you shall chase an hundred, and an hundred of you shall put ten thousand to flight: and your enemies shall fall before you by the sword."

Logic tells us that one hundred soldiers with swords are not going to make ten thousand enemy soldiers with similar weapons run away unless they have a type of superior weaponry, something similar to Moses's "rod of God" or Joshua's "spear."

Section 23
How Did Jehovah's Angel Kill 185,000 Soldiers in Their Sleep?

In Second Kings 19:35, Jehovah sends an angel to kill 185,000 Assyrian soldiers as they sleep in their camp. How can one angel kill 185,000 armed soldiers as they sleep without someone waking up and sounding the alarm? One practical explanation is that these 185,000 soldiers were sprayed with poison gas by a type of silent aircraft as they slept.

CHAPTER 6

JEHOVAH IS AN INSTIGATOR OF EVIL

Section 1
Jehovah Uses Evil Spirits to Instigate Evil

In Judges 9:23–24, Jehovah sent an evil spirit to promote treachery between humans, "Then God sent an evil spirit between Abimelech and the men of Shechem, and the men of Shechem dealt treacherously with Abimelech." The evil spirit sent by Jehovah instigated murder among brothers.

Jehovah also sent evil spirits to harass people as written in First Samuel 16:14–15, "But the Spirit of the Lord departed from Saul, and an evil spirit from the Lord troubled him. And Saul's servants said unto him, Behold now, an evil spirit from God troubleth thee."

It is clear that these evil spirits are from Jehovah, not from Satan. In First Samuel 19:9–10, Jehovah sends an evil spirit that has Saul attempt to kill the future king David. In Isaiah 19:14, Jehovah sends a perverse spirit to cause trouble in Egypt.

So why would Jehovah send an evil spirit to manipulate Saul to attempt to kill David, the future king of Israel? Why does the biblical god instigate evil then punishes by instigating more evil? Perhaps Jehovah feeds off the pain and misery he causes among people. Maybe this is how he entertains himself. It stands to reason that this biblical god is the origin of all the evil, pain, and suffering encountered throughout the Bible narrative and perhaps also in today's modern societies.

Another example of Jehovah commanding evil spirits as part of his process of orchestrating events is found in First Kings. In this account, Jehovah wants to get rid of King Ahab and is asking for a volunteer who will help him manipulate King Ahab into a situation that would lead to his murder. The entities he is conversing with include an evil spirit that volunteers to help Jehovah orchestrate the evil event by causing King Ahab's prophets to lie as written in First Kings 22:20–23:

> And the Lord said, Who shall persuade Ahab, that he may go up and fall at Ramothgilead?
>
> And there came forth a spirit, and stood before the Lord, and said, I will persuade him.
>
> And the Lord said unto him, Wherewith? And he said, I will go forth, and I will be a lying spirit in the mouth of all his prophets. And he said, Thou shalt persuade him, and prevail also: go forth, and do so.
>
> Now therefore, behold, the Lord hath put a lying spirit in the mouth of all these thy prophets, and the Lord hath spoken evil concerning thee.

How much clearer can it get that Jehovah is the source of evil throughout the biblical scripture narrative? How can anyone deny this after reading it for themselves? It is clear that Jehovah is initiating and manipulating evil in order to orchestrate the behavior of the people. Jehovah manipulates the prophets of King Ahab of Israel to lie by using evil spirits to make them lie. This is done to give Ahab false information that would persuade him to go into Ramothgilead where he would be killed. All these events are being orchestrated by Jehovah and his evil spirits.

Jehovah boasts about the severity of the evil he brings in Second Kings 21:12, "Therefore thus saith the Lord God of Israel, Behold, I am bringing such evil upon Jerusalem and Judah, that whosoever heareth of it, both his ears shall tingle."

Section 2
Jehovah, His Angels, and Evil Spirits Are like
Parasitical Demons and Psychic Vampires

Much of the book of Judges is filled with accounts of Jehovah orchestrating events for the Israelites to be taken into captivity then freed when he decides to free them. Thousands of them are killed while they kill thousands themselves in the course of these events.

Consider all the negative emotions that these violent events cause—emotions such as fear, hate, sorrow, anguish, etc. As we follow the biblical narrative, it becomes clear that the orchestrator of these events is Jehovah himself. He manipulates Pharaoh several times into changing his mind about freeing the Israelites by "hardening his heart," which prolongs the pain and suffering of the people especially the Egyptians. He also similarly orchestrates other events that also lead to much pain and suffering for people.

Despite all the physical and psychological abuse orchestrated by Jehovah against the Israelites and other people, we read the following prayer in Isaiah 25:1, "O Lord, thou art my God; I will exalt thee, I will praise thy name; for thou hast done wonderful things; thy counsels of old are faithfulness and truth." I suggest that one possible explanation for such total submission expressed in this prayer after the cruel treatment by Jehovah is that it is the result of the physical and psychological trauma the Israelites were subjected to by Jehovah. It is like when one who is being tortured says anything the torturer wants to hear to stop the torture.

I suggest this trauma was inflicted by Jehovah on the Israelites as part of the process of taking control of their collective minds by instilling the fear-of-God trait into their collective consciousness and perhaps even their collective unconsciousness. This fear is then passed down from generation to generation. Perhaps this fear is not only passed from generation to generation through culture and religious dogma but also through DNA (Bahjat 2017).

The biblical narrative infers that evil spirits are directly connected to and work under the direction of Jehovah, and together, they orchestrate events that eventually lead to the great pain and suffering of humanity. It is as if Jehovah feeds off of the misery he orchestrates among humans, similar to the cosmic predator described in Carlos Castaneda's book entitled *The Active Side of Infinity*. The following are excerpts from his book that describes this predator:

> We have a predator that came from the depths of the cosmos and took over the rule of our lives. Human beings are its prisoners. The predator is our lord and master. It has rendered us docile, helpless. If we want to protest, it suppresses our protest. If we want to act independently, it demands that we don't do so . . . They took over because we are food for them, and they squeeze us mercilessly because we are their sustenance. Just as we rear chickens in chicken coops, *gallineros*, the predators rear us in human coops, *humaneros*. Therefore, their food is always available to them . . . the predators have given us our systems of beliefs, our ideas of good and evil, our social mores. They are the ones who set up our hopes and expectations and dreams of success or failure. They have given us covetousness, greed, and cowardice. It is the predators who make us complacent, routinary, and egomaniacal . . . In order to keep us obedient and meek and weak . . . They gave us their mind! Do you hear me? The predators give us their mind, which becomes our mind. The predators mind is baroque, contradictory, morose, filled with the fear of being discovered any minute now. Through the mind, which, after all, is their mind, the predators inject into the lives of human beings whatever is convenient for them. And they ensure, in this manner, a degree of security to act as a buffer against their fear" (Castaneda, 1998, pp. 218–220).

The predators in Castaneda's book parallel Jehovah and his organization of Satan, evil spirits, and angels in the narrative of the Judeo-Christian Bible. Jehovah and his organization are the predators and humans are the prey that have been captured and corralled through the systems of religion, politics, and money, which have transformed us into the metaphoric domesticated farm animals that we are compared and referred to throughout the Bible.

Section 3
Jehovah Collaborates with His Sons and Satan

In the book of Job, there is a meeting between Jehovah, his sons, and Satan in what appears to be a debriefing. It seems to be a meeting where the sons of Jehovah and Satan are reporting to Jehovah about things on earth. It alludes to the collaboration between Jehovah and Satan. The following is an excerpt from this meeting that is described in Job 1-7:

> "Again, there was a day when the sons of God came to present themselves before the Lord, and Satan came also among them to present himself before the Lord. And the Lord said unto Satan, Whence comest thou: Then Satan answered the Lord, and said, From going to and fro in the earth, and from walking up and down in it.
>
> And the Lord said unto Satan, Hast thou considered my servant Job, that there is none like him in the earth, a perfect and an upright man, one that feareth God, and escheweth evil? And still he holdeth fast his integrity, although thou movedst me against him, to destroy him without cause.
>
> And Satan answered the Lord, and said, Skin for skin yea, all that a man hath will he give for his life.
>
> But put forth thine hand now, and touch his bone and flesh, and he will curse thee to thy face.

And the Lord said unto Satan, Behold, he is in thine hand; but save his life.

So went Satan forth from the presence of the Lord, and smote Job with sore boils from the sole of his foot unto his crown."

In the above narrative, Jehovah asked Satan where he had been. Satan answered casually that he had been up and down the earth. In the course of their conversation, Jehovah appeared to be boasting about the faithfulness and obedience of his servant Job. Then Jehovah and Satan collaborated to test the obedience Job has to Jehovah much like when Jehovah tested Abraham's obedience in Genesis. In other words, Jehovah wanted to test the thoroughness of his mind control of Job, and he used Satan to do so. As part of their collaboration, Jehovah told Satan he could do anything to Job, his family, and property except kill him. Satan began by afflicting Job with sore boils from the bottom of his feet to the top of his head.

Section 4
The Book of Job Is about a Wager between Jehovah and Satan

The story of Job underscores the following concerning Jehovah of the Bible: (1) Jehovah demands fear and sees it as a virtue, (2) Jehovah demands regular blood sacrifice, (3) Jehovah has more than one son, (4) Jehovah and Satan collaborate to manipulate individual humans and to orchestrate human events, (5) Jehovah places little value on human life, and (6) Jehovah's main concern is complete control of human behavior.

The story of Job begins with the narrator commentating how obedient and fearful of Jehovah the character Job is. He is described as "perfect and upright." He regularly presents burnt offerings (blood sacrifice) to Jehovah for himself and his sons.

Then during a meeting between Jehovah, his sons, and Satan, Jehovah seems to be bragging to Satan how perfect and obedient Job is. Satan responds that the reason for that was because Jehovah favored and protected him and he had an easy life.

Then in what appears to be a wager between Jehovah and Satan, Jehovah agrees to let Satan make Job's life miserable to see if he remains loyal to him. In the biblical account, Jehovah lets Satan kill Job's sons, servants, and livestock among other miseries he causes him. At the end of the story, Jehovah's complete mind control of Job is obvious, and Jehovah rewards him by giving him greater wealth than he had before. It appears that Jehovah won the bet with Satan.

According to the biblical narrative, Jehovah, his sons, Satan, and evil spirits are all on the same team. Again, they collaborate with Jehovah as their leader to control and manipulate human behavior and events.

Another example of collaboration between Satan and Jehovah is found in First Chronicles chapter 21, where Satan provokes David to "number Israel." Jehovah then responds by bringing a plague upon Israel that kills seventy thousand men. As written in First Chronicles 21:1, 21:7, and 21:14:

> And Satan stood up against Israel, and provoked David to number Israel.
>
> And God was displeased with this thing; therefore he smote Israel.
>
> So the Lord sent pestilence against Israel: and there fell of Israel seventy thousand men.

To paraphrase, Jehovah allows Satan to manipulate King David, who displeases him. Instead of smiting or punishing Satan or King David, Jehovah kills seventy thousand men with disease. It stands to reason that Jehovah sent Satan to manipulate his servant King David as he had sent Satan to manipulate his other servant Job. This is another of many examples throughout the Judeo-Christian Bible of Jehovah orchestrating events that result in his killing of tens of thousands of people at a time. He does not hesitate to kill Israelites as well as non-Israelites.

Section 5
Jehovah Manipulates People to Betray and Murder Each Other

In Second Kings chapter 8, King Benhadad of Syria became sick. He heard that the prophet Elisha, who had brought a dead boy back to life, is in Damascus. The king sent someone named Hazael with gifts and a question for Elisha. Hazael asked the prophet Elisha if the king would recover from his disease. Elisha told Hazael that Jehovah had shown him that the king was going to die but to tell him that he would recover. Elisha then began to cry, and Hazael asked him why he was crying. The prophet Elisha told him it was because he knew the evil that he was going to do to the people of Israel, including murdering children and ripping up pregnant women.

Hazael then returned to the king and lied to him as directed by the prophet Elisha. He told him that he would recover but then murdered him and took over the kingship and proceeded to do the evil that Jehovah wanted him to do. The account can be read in Second Kings 8:10–15.

Here again, Jehovah is instigating events that lead to political assassination in that Hazael murders the king in his bed and then becomes king himself. At the same time, Jehovah has also instigated a war that will include slaughtering children and ripping up pregnant women.

Section 6
Jehovah Commands the Israelites to Genocide Each Other

Jehovah instigated wars of genocide among the different Israeli families. He had his prophets anoint kings so they could attack other established kings who he wanted to punish. This punishment may include extinguishing their bloodline.

For example, in Second Kings chapters 9 and 10, Jehovah's plan to exterminate King Ahab's bloodline came to fruition. By this time,

Jehovah and his collaborators, including his prophets, had created a situation where various kings were competing for power.

Joram was the king of Israel, but on orders from Jehovah, Elisha the prophet had one of his helpers anoint Jehu king of Israel. Jehu sent letters to government officials and elders in Samaria to persuade them to betray the seventy sons of the late King Ahab. Some of these government officials and elders had helped raise these seventy sons of King Ahab; nevertheless, they agreed to betray them. Then the extermination began as written in Second Kings 10:7–11:

> And it came to pass, when the letter came to them, that they took the king's sons, and slew seventy persons, and put their heads in baskets, and sent him them to Jezreel . . . So Jehu slew all that remained of the house of Ahab in Jezreel, and all his great men, and his kinsfolks, and his priests, until he left him none remaining.

So again, Jehovah, the man of war and god of Israel, uses Israelis to commit genocide on other Israelis.

Section 7
Jehovah Proclaims That He Brings Evil

In the following verses, Jehovah describes and boasts of some of the evil things he has done and will do in the future as you can read in Second Kings 21:12, Jeremiah 19:3, Jeremiah 44:2, Jeremiah 44:27, and Jeremiah 46:10. He describes evil that will be so heinous it will make people's ears tingle when they hear about it. Genocide through war is referred to as a sacrifice. These are examples of the biblical narrative affirming that the so-called god of the Bible is the opposite of a just and loving god. According to the biblical narrative, Jehovah is evil and unjust.

Section 8
Jehovah Manipulates Babylon to Kill Israelis and Egyptians Then Manipulates Other Peoples to Kill the Babylonians

After Jehovah uses Babylon to cause death and destruction against Israel and Egypt, he uses other nations to do the same to Babylon. This is described in Jeremiah 43:10–11. Jehovah describes the Babylonian king Nebuchadnezzar as his servant. There are Jews living in Egypt at this time, so Jehovah orders the king of Babylon to conquer Egypt to punish these Jews for not following his commands. In other words, Jehovah is killing Egyptians as part of his process to kill Jews as written in Jeremiah 44:12, "And I will take the remnant of Judah, that have set their faces to go into the land of Egypt to sojourn there, and they shall all be consumed . . . by the sword and by the famine."

Jehovah then punishes Babylon, who he had recently referred to as his servant, by manipulating other nations to attack her. This account can be read in Jeremiah 50:9. Again, Jehovah creates chaos and misery by manipulating nations to fight against one another.

Section 9
Jehovah Becomes Angry at King Saul for Showing Mercy

More bloodthirsty behavior exhibited by Jehovah is found in First Samuel chapter 15 where he commands Saul to attack the Amalekites and kill all men, women, children, including infants, and all the animals. Then he becomes angry because Saul spared the king of the Amalekites and some of the animals. This account can be read in First Samuel 15:3, 15:7–9, and 15:10–11. To correct Saul's disobedience, the prophet Samuel has King Agag, whose life King Saul had spared, brought to him and then hacks him to pieces in front of Jehovah.

Samuel reemphasizes Jehovah's demand for complete, unquestioned obedience when he tells Saul that Jehovah puts more importance on obedience than sacrifice as written in First Samuel 15:22, "Behold, to obey is better than sacrifice, and to hearken than the fat of rams." In other words, God's main emphasis and demand is total unquestioning mind control.

Section 10
Jehovah Sends an Evil Spirit That Influences King Saul to Attempt to Murder His Son-in-Law David, the Future King of Israel

Much of the first book of Samuel is a saga about the first king of Israel named Saul attempting to kill the future second king of Israel named David. Included in this saga is a whole bunch of killings, including women and children.

In his pursuit of David, Saul is killing anybody that he suspects of helping David hide from him including the priests of their god Jehovah, their entire families including children and infants, and all their animals. Some of these accounts are described in First Samuel 19:9–10 and 22:17–19.

Section 11
Jehovah, Satan, Angels, Devils, and Jesus Are All Interrelated

According to the book of Revelation 12:9, dragon, serpent, devil, and Satan seem to be the same entity, "And the great dragon was cast out, that old serpent, called the Devil, and Satan." The narrator says the great dragon is an old serpent sometimes called the devil and Satan. Those are four different terms for the same entity. According to Second Esdras 15:29, there are many dragons from more than one nation, "Where the nations of the dragons of Arabia shall come out with many chariots."

According to the biblical narrative, it stands to reason that there are many dragons, serpents, devils, and Satan. The terms are referring to the same or similar entities. And as told in the story of Job and other accounts in the Bible, they collaborate with Jehovah to manipulate and control people. I suggest they all belong to the same or similar organizations as Jehovah I also suggest that the terms *dragon, devil, Satan,* and *serpent* in the Bible literature may be referring to reptilian humanoids. Furthermore, I suggest that Jehovah and all the aforementioned entities in the Old and New Testaments including Jesus, angels, evil spirits, and prophets may also all be part of the same or similar organizations. Their main objective is to maintain control of the minds of humanity and human behavior necessary in maintaining the aforementioned systems of religion, politics, and money.

Recall that in Genesis, the entity that encouraged Eve to eat from the tree of knowledge was a serpent (reptilian). This same entity is also referred to as Satan (reptilian) or the devil (reptilian) throughout the Bible. In the book of Job, Jehovah has a meeting with his sons and Satan, then he sends Satan to cause misery on Job. Second Esdras describes dragons (reptilians) coming out with chariots "carried as the wind upon the earth" to engage in battle with humans as allies and adversaries. I suggest that Jehovah may also be a type of reptilian humanoid. The following accounts describe battles between reptilian entities and humans.

Second Esdras 15:28–31 says,

> Behold an horrible vision, and the appearance thereof from the east: Where the many nations of the dragons of Arabia shall come out with many chariots, and the multitude of them shall be carried as the wind upon earth, that all they which hear them may fear and tremble. Also the Carmanians raging in wrath shall go forth as the wild boars of the wood, and with great power shall they come, and join battle with them, and shall waste a portion of the land of the Assyrians. And then shall the dragons have the upper hand, remembering their nature; and if they shall turn themselves, conspiring together in great power to persecute them.

It is inferred that these dragons are traveling in flying vehicles referred to as chariots carried as the wind upon earth and are allied with a group of humans (Carmanians) and fight against and defeat another group of humans (Assyrians). After defeating the Assyrians, the dragons remember their nature and turn on their human allies.

Also in Second Esdras, the narrator describes a battle in the sky between flying vehicles described as clouds and stars where many of the stars are sent crashing to earth. These vehicles are using weapons described as "fire and hail, and flying swords." They are also attacking the cities. The narrator does not say who is piloting these crafts, but one probability is that some of them are piloted by the aforementioned reptilians. Some of these accounts are described in the book of Second Esdras 15:34–35 and 15:38–44. Example:

> Behold clouds from the east and from the north unto the south, and they are very horrible to look upon, full of wrath and storm. They shall smite one upon another, and they shall smite down a great multitude of stars upon the earth, even their own star . . . Fire and hail, and flying sword . . . And they shall break down the cities and walls.

As mentioned before, the narrator of these biblical accounts is describing advanced technology that our education system today teaches did not exist at that time. I presume that the biblical narrator did not have words to describe machine-gun fire with tracer bullets nor rockets, missiles, lasers, and other types of modern weaponry, so they used descriptive words such as "fire and hail, and flying swords."

The book of Revelation chapter 12 describes a battle in heaven (the sky) where a dragon knocks down a bunch of stars from the sky and sends them crashing to earth as written in Revelation 12:3–4: "And there appeared another wonder in heaven; and behold a great red dragon . . . And his tail drew the third part of the stars of heaven, and did cast them to the earth."

Today the same account of stars of heaven and the great red dragon might be described as a battle in the sky between a huge red UFO and a bunch of smaller UFOs where the huge UFO disables a bunch of the smaller ones and sends them crashing to earth.

In Judges 5:19–20, stars from heaven fought against the Canaanite army—"They fought from heaven; the stars in their courses fought against Sisera."

Note that in the above verse, Sisera is the commander of a Canaanite army who was fighting against vehicles in the sky that were referred to as stars from heaven. These stars may be the same chariots of fire or bright objects descending from the sky referred to in other parts of the Bible such as Second Kings, Second Esdras, Ezekiel chapter 1, and Isaiah 66:15.

Who are the kings who came and fought mentioned in the above verse 19? Are they from the nations of the dragons of Arabia previously mentioned in Second Esdras 15:29? The dragons described in Second Esdras are clearly inferring intelligent beings that are organized into nations and are traveling in vehicles described as clouds and chariots. They are fighting against humans on earth and other entities that are also traveling in vehicles described as clouds, chariots, and stars from heaven.

Perhaps the aforementioned organization or organizations of Jehovah, Satan, angels, demons, and prophets are fighting among one another for control of land and humanity. This would parallel the historical and contemporary imperial nations of the world fighting against one another also for the control of land and humanity.

Jehovah sometimes also travels in a cloud as written in Exodus 18:9, "And the Lord said unto Moses, Lo, I come unto thee in a thick cloud." Another example of Jehovah's mode of travel is in Exodus 13:21, where he travels in a pillar of a cloud and in a pillar of fire. In Second Samuel 22:11, where King David is being rescued from his enemies, he describes Jehovah as riding on a cherub.[21] Is a cherub actually a metaphor for an aircraft that Jehovah rides in?

---

[21]   A celestial being

In Revelation 9:1, a star that falls from the sky is given the key to the bottomless pit. Could this falling star be a metaphor for the landing of an aircraft?

In Revelation 10:1, John describes an angel that was in a cloud with the colors of a rainbow and as bright as the sun.

In Matthew 17:5, while Jesus is speaking, Jehovah arrives in and speaks from a bright cloud.

In Acts 9:3–5, Jesus is described as a bright light in heaven that converses with a traveler on the road to Damascus. Is Jesus actually speaking from inside a bright aircraft that today would be referred to as a UFO?

There is a definite correlation in the mode of travel of devils, angels, Jehovah, and Jesus as described in the above examples. They travel in clouds, pillars of fire, bright lights, stars, and chariots of fire as described by the prophets Elijah (Second Kings 2:11), Elisha (Second Kings 6:17), and Ezekiel (chapter 8). I suggest that the original observer is using metaphors in his descriptions of the vehicles he observes. These vehicles attack one another and occasionally a bunch of them described as stars are sent crashing to earth. There are obvious battles going on in the sky that include humans on the ground. I suggest that the battles in the sky are between different factions of gods, angels, devils, Satans, serpents, dragons, and humans. I also suggest that they may be fighting a high-tech war for control of earth and its people.

Is there a parallel between heavenly entities and their worshipers on earth? Perhaps, in their imperial invasions of the various indigenous peoples of the world, the various European groups copied the behavior of their gods. Just as the different factions of gods, angels, Satans, serpents, and dragons use the different groups of humans against one another in their battles for control, and so did the European invaders use the indigenous peoples of the world against one another in their battles for control of land and people.

Perhaps the aforementioned accounts describing battles involving celestial beings and earthlings for control of land and people have been a constant throughout documented human history.

CHAPTER 7

JEHOVAH DEMANDS HUMAN BABIES AND ANIMALS BE SACRIFICED TO HIM

Section 1
All the Firstborn Are Sacrificed to Jehovah

In Numbers 3:13, Jehovah reminded Moses that the firstborn of the Israelites and their animals belong to him because he killed the firstborn children and animals of the Egyptians as part of the process of leading them out of Egypt. He emphasized that he is the Lord as a justification for doing whatever he feels like doing to them and their families.

Moses was again reminded of their debt to Jehovah in Numbers 8:17, "For all the firstborn of the children of Israel are mine, both man and beast: on the day that I smote every firstborn in the land of Egypt I sanctified them for myself."

Section 2
Blood Rituals Described in the Old Testament
Parallel Contemporary Satanic Blood Rituals

Exodus 24:5–8 describes blood rituals that today would be described as satanic.

> And Moses took half of the blood, and put it in basons;
> and half of the blood he sprinkled on the altar. And he
> took the book of the covenant, and read in the audience
> of the people and they said, All that the Lord hath said
> will we do, and be obedient. And Moses took the blood,
> and sprinkled it on the people, and said, Behold the
> blood of the covenant, which the Lord hath made with
> you concerning all these words.

The account sounds like a creepy ritualistic scene from a satanic movie.

In Genesis 15:8–12, Jehovah had Abraham conduct a creepy ritual where Abraham was required to kill a turtledove and a young pigeon. He was also required to mutilate a young cow, a goat, and a ram. This was required by Jehovah as part of a covenantwhere he promised a bunch of land to Abraham and his descendants. The account does not mention the fact that this promised land was already inhabited by the indigenous peoples of that land.

In another strange blood sacrifice, Moses was commanded by God to kill a ram and put its blood on the tip of his brother's right ear, his right thumb, and his big toe on the right foot. He did the same to Aaron's sons and then sprinkled some of the blood around the altar (Leviticus 8:22–24).

The book of Leviticus is full of various blood rituals as atonement for different types of sins. The blood is taken by killing animals such as turtledoves, pigeons, lambs, goats, rams, and bullocks.[22] Leviticus 14: 50–53 describes cleansing a house by taking the blood of a bird and sprinkling it on the house seven times.

An example of humans being used as blood sacrifices, also known as burnt offerings, to appease Jehovah is described in the book of Judges. The character Jephthah told Jehovah he would sacrifice to him the first person who comes out of his house when he returns from war if Jehovah helps him conquer the people of Ammon.

---

[22]   Young bulls

After Jephthah conquered Ammon with Jehovah's assistance, he arrived at his house and the first person who came out of his house to greet him was his daughter, who was his only child. This is an indication that human sacrifice of one's children was not uncommon among the ancient Israelites. Who else was Jephthah expecting to come out of his house to greet him, his wife?

In plain language, Jephthah murdered his only child and burned her body as a blood sacrifice to an entity that had convinced him and others like him that he is their god. This is his payment to the man of war, a god called Jehovah, for helping him kill other humans in war.

Another blatant example of human sacrifice is seen in Second Samuel chapter 21. Here, King David asked the Gibeonites how he could make atonement for King Saul's violation of a covenant that had been made between the Israelites and the Gibeonite people. King Saul had been dead for years at this time. King David agreed to give them seven of King Saul's sons so they may be sacrificed to Jehovah. The account can be read in Second Samuel 21:3 and 21:5–9.

As you will see later in this book, the practice of murdering humans as sacrifices to Jehovah continues today among some people who belong to the Abrahamic religions of Judaism, Christianity, and Islam.

The Israelites were not the only people in the Middle East who sacrifice people and animals to their god. After Israel attacks the Moabites following the command of Jehovah, the king of the Moabites sacrifices his eldest son to his god Chemosh for the help against the Israelites and their god Jehovah. This account can be read in Second Kings 3:26–27.

Section 3
The Jews Initiate Christianity by Crucifying Jesus

Christianity began when the Jews sacrificed Jesus. Today this human blood sacrifice is called the crucifixion and is symbolically exhibited in all Christian churches. According to the Bible, the founders of the Christian church began accumulating wealth by taking it from its members under the penalty of death as described in Acts chapters 4 and

5. The Christian church accumulated a massive amount of wealth as the official religion of the Roman Empire and continued this accumulation of wealth after the fall of Rome when it became the most powerful political and religious organization in Europe.

The Christian church was the main organization in organizing the various European peoples into political units called kingdoms and then countries. This was accomplished through many years of bloody wars usually referred to as holy wars. These wars generated a massive amount of human blood sacrifice, which undoubtedly was very pleasing to their war god Jehovah. This accumulation of wealth and control through war by the Christian church continued through the Crusades and European invasions of the Americas.

When the Portuguese, Spanish, and British Empires began waging war against the rest of the peoples of the world to spread Christianity and accumulate wealth, the Christian church received its share of the gold, silver, and other forms of wealth, which included control of people and land. It is not by coincidence that the Christian priests always accompanied the Spanish conquistadors in their quests for wealth. They were sent by the Roman Catholic Church to keep record of the wealth being plundered and the inhabitants of the lands.

After the Jews and Christians, the Islamic Ottoman Empire was the third imperialist Abrahamic religion to spread its influence around as much of the globe as it could. When we trace the historical narrative of the Jewish, Christian, and Islamic religions, it becomes obvious that all three are rooted in the same god of war presented as the dominant god of the Judeo-Christian Bible and the Islamic Koran. "The Lord is a man of war: the Lord is his name" (Exodus 15:3).

Fast-forward to modern history and we see the modern empire of the United States become the wealthiest and most powerful country in the world through war, especially World Wars I and II; which is when the military industrial complex was firmly established as part of the US economy. *Military industrial complex* is the term President Eisenhower used to describe the collaboration between the military, corporations, politicians, and financial institutions to keep the US in a perpetual state of war specifically for monetary gain. This idea of war for profit was actually written about after World War I. The term used to describe the US industries that significantly increased their profits during that war was *merchants of death*. They are alive and well to this day.

All the known empires throughout human history became empires through war, which is a vehicle for human blood sacrifice. Abraham was manipulated to offer his only child as a blood sacrifice to prove his fear and obedience to Jehovah. Jephthah offered his only child to the same god for victory in war. Even today, there are parents that parallel this type of thinking when they consider the death and maiming of their sons and daughters as an honor if it happens while serving in the military. They perceive this as a sacrifice for their country. It is more accurately a blood sacrifice to the military industrial complex[23] and to Jehovah, the man of war.

Two-time Medal of Honor recipient US Marine General Smedley Butler considered war an insidious and deceitful way to reap economic benefits for owners of corporations and banks, which he said make huge profits through war. He also stated that this would not be possible without the cooperation of the political system. He emphasized this throughout his book *War Is a Racket* (Butler, 1936). He also describes how he eventually realized he was just a hitman for the wealthy owners of US corporations such as oil, banking, transportation, communication, and others that promote war for profit. He describes how the leaders of the industry and the military would meet with political leaders at lavish social gatherings to discuss business.

Section 4
Jehovah's Lust for Blood and Violence Is Insatiable

The Old Testament is bathed in the blood of men, women, children, and animals. In Isaiah 34:5–6, Jehovah described his lust for human and animal blood:

---

[23] Collusion between a nation's armed forces, industries that supply them, financial institutions, and politicians whose motive is maintaining a war economy for personal economic gain.

For my sword shall be bathed in heaven: behold, it shall come down upon Idumea, and upon the people of my curse, to judgment. The sword of the Lord is filled with blood, it is made fat with fatness, and with the blood of lambs and goats, with the fat of the kidneys of rams: for the Lord hath a sacrifice in Bozrah, and a great slaughter in the land of Idumea.

In other words, Jehovah was saying that all the killing of humans and animals was his curse manifested through blood sacrifice of humans and animals. He achieved the massive sacrifice of humans by instigating and manipulating wars. The "sacrifice in Bozrah" and "great slaughter in the land of Idumea" infer mass killings of humans.

The mind-boggling thing is that after he killed the people, their children, and animals, Jehovah expected to be worshipped and adored and demanded more blood sacrifice! There were more punishments and killings when the blood sacrifices demanded in the covenants were not completed as specified. The Israelites were told to be grateful for this treatment because they were his chosen people. They were practically chosen to be his mind-controlled slaves.

In Isaiah 46:9, this self-proclaimed god pronounced how great and awesome he was, "Remember the former things of old: for I am God, and there is none else; I am God, and there is none like me." There is a sense of an overinflated ego that may be described with words such as *vain*, *narcissistic*, and *arrogant*. These are just more examples of the negative human qualities of Jehovah.

Section 5
A Man Cuts Up His Dead Wife into Twelve Pieces and Sends Her All over Israel to Initiate War between the Various Tribes

An example of the insanity that occurs in some of the narratives in the Bible, the Old Testament in particular, is described in Judges chapter 19. A man who was only identified as "a certain Levite" went after his concubine[24] after she had left him to stay with her father. On the way back from her father's house, they spent the night at a place called Gibeah. They stayed at the house of an old man who lived there with his daughter. During the night, some male sexual deviants from the city knocked on the door and wanted to have sex with the Levite, but the old man offered his daughter and the Levite's concubine instead (not very chivalrous). The men were reluctant at first, but the Levite convinced them to take his concubine instead of him (also not very chivalrous). So they took and "abused" her all nightlong, and the next morning, the Levite found her dead outside the front door. He then put her on a donkey and headed back home. After they arrived at his house, he took a knife and cut up her corpse into twelve pieces and sent them all over Israel.

What kind of madness is this? This type of psychopathic behavior should come as no surprise if we consider the entity this man calls God and the ritual blood sacrifices this so-called God demands throughout the Bible. The incident led to a war between two groups of Israelites, the tribe of Benjamin versus the other tribes of Israel, which resulted in the death of 65,100 Israelites. Apparently, the Levite's wife was killed on the land of the tribe of Benjamin.

After defeating the tribe of Benjamin, the other tribes of Israel went and killed all the men, women, and children of the inhabitants of Jabeshgilead because they did not help fight against the tribe of Benjamin. They did spare and capture four hundred young virgins.

---

[24] Secondary wife (Elwell, 1997)

CHAPTER 8

EXTRATERRESTRIALS OR TECHNOLOGICALLY ADVANCED HUMANS?

Section 1
200 Angels Land on Earth to Have Sex with Human Females

The book of the prophet Enoch is not included in most Bible versions because it is considered noncanonical[25] literature. However, Enoch is mentioned in Genesis that he walked with God and was Noah's great-grandfather (Genesis 5:22–29).

One of the many things Enoch described in the book of Enoch was the landing of two hundred angels on the summit of Mount Hermon to have sex with human females. If this event were to happen today, the two hundred angels would be referred to as two hundred extraterrestrials as written in the book of Enoch chapter 6 versus 1–6:

> And it came to pass when the children of men had
> multiplied that in those were born unto them beautiful

---

25   Not included in the list of sacred books accepted as genuine by religious authorities

and comely[26] daughters. And the angels, the children of the heaven, saw and lusted after them, and said to one another: Come, let us choose us wives from among the children of men and beget us children. And Semjaza, who was their leader, said unto them: I fear ye will not indeed agree to do this deed, and I alone shall have to pay the penalty of a great sin. And they all answered him and said: Let us all swear an oath, and all bind ourselves by mutual imprecations[27] not to abandon this plan but to do this thing. Then sware they all together and bound themselves by mutual imprecations upon it. And they were all in all two hundred; who descended in the days of Jared on the summit of Mount Hermon.

The narrative clearly describes entities in the sky observing and finding the women on earth very attractive. These entities are referred to as angels, and the sky is referred to as heaven. Their lust for these women becomes so great that two hundred of them make an agreement to land on earth and take these women as wives. Their leader, Semjaza, reminds the others that they are breaking the law of the organization they belong to. Nevertheless, they all make an agreement to satisfy their desire to have sex with the earth women. They do this after holding some type of ritual that includes swearing an oath and binding themselves by mutual imprecations (spoken curses). They then land in their aircraft on Mount Hermon and proceed to breed with the earth women. According to the narrative, the angels are "physical beings that behave very much like men." It stands to reason that they are physically the same or similar to men in that they have physical sex with women, just as the sons of God do in Genesis.

Throughout the book of Enoch, he described many things that were shown to him in the heavens by different angels. Even though the book

---

26 Attractive

27 Spoken curses

of Enoch is a noncanonical book, similar accounts are referred to in the canonical[28] book of Genesis. For example:

Genesis 6:2. "That the sons of God saw the daughters of men that they were fair; and they took them wives of all which they chose."

Genesis 6:4. "There were giants in the earth in those days; and also after that, when the sons of God came in unto the daughters of men, and they bare children to them."

Section 2
The Prophet Ezekiel Describes a Flying Craft Containing Humanoids That Take Him Up into the Sky

The prophet Ezekiel described a flying machine that four humanlike creatures emerged from as written in Ezekiel 1:4–5:

> And I looked, and, behold, a whirlwind came out of
> the north, a great cloud, and a fire infolding itself, and
> a brightness was about it, and out of the midst thereof
> as the colour of amber . . . Also out of the midst thereof
> came the likeness of four living creatures. And this was
> their appearance; they had the likeness of a man.

The above account brings to mind the scene from the movie *Close Encounters of the Third Kind* when the alien craft arrive within infolding clouds and bright, colorful lights. After the craft lands and the mist subside, humanoid beings and humans who had been previously abducted emerge from the craft. Ezekiel clearly describes four entities that look like men come out of the flying craft that he described.

In Ezekiel 8:1–3 and 11:1, he describes what today may be interpreted as an alien abduction:

---

[28] A list of sacred books considered genuine by religious authorities.

As I sat in mine house, and the elders of Judah sat before me, that the hand of the Lord GOD fell there upon me. Then I beheld, and lo a likeness as the appearance of fire: from the appearances of his loins even downward, fire: and from his loins even upward, as the appearance of brightness, as the colour of amber. "And he put forth the form of an hand, and took me by a lock of mine head; and the spirit lifted me up between the earth and the heaven . . . to the door of the inner gate that looketh toward the north.

Moreover the spirit lifted me up, and brought me unto the east gate of the Lord's house.

The prophet Ezekiel is describing being taken up to the sky by something he describes as bright and colorful out of which came four manlike beings and the form of a hand that takes hold of him and lifts him into the sky. He also says that he was taken to the "Lord's house." He is aware of his cardinal directions in that he distinguishes between an inner gate that faces north, and the east gate of the structure he calls "the Lord's house."

Was the Lord's house a giant aircraft?

Section 3
The Prophet Elijah Had Foreknowledge He Would Be Taken Up in an Aircraft

According to the biblical narrative, the prophet Elijah knew that he was going to be taken away by Jehovah. What made Elijah's circumstances more curious is that there were several individuals referred to as sons of the prophets who knew the day he would be taken. Elijah's assistant and apprentice Elisha also was aware that Elijah was going to be taken by Jehovah, as described in Second Kings 2:3.

Elijah was aware that he was going to be taken away by Jehovah or agents of Jehovah. This was apparent in a conversation between himself and Elisha as they were traveling together. This was described in Second Kings 2:9–10.

The entities referred to as God and his angels were apparently in communication with Elijah, his apprentice Elisha, and the group called sons of the prophets. They all seemed to be communicating directly with Jehovah and his so-called angels.

Elijah was eventually taken up into the sky by a flying craft that was described as a "chariot of fire" and a "whirlwind." The account can be read in Second Kings 2:11–14.

What seemed strange in the departure of Elijah was that the only thing left behind was his mantle, which Elisha retrieved at the site of his abduction. Elisha promptly used it to part the waters of the River Jordan as Elijah had done before. This mantle was obviously not an ordinary piece of garment. After Elijah's abduction, Elisha began wearing the mantle and replaced him as prophet.

Comments made by the members of the sons of the prophets indicate that they were concerned that the ones who had taken Elijah may have left him on a mountain or in a valley. They refer to whatever or whoever took Elijah as the Spirit of the Lord. They also took fifty men and searched for Elijah for three days but could not find him. The inference was given that they had experienced or witnessed similar events before where the person taken into the sky had been deposited in remote locations. In this case, however, Elijah was not seen again. The account may be read in Second Kings 2:16– The following is an excerpt from this section:

> Let them go, we pray thee, and seek thy master: lest
> peradventure the Spirit of the Lord hath taken him up,
> and cast him upon some mountain, or into some valley.

After taking over the duties of the prophet, Elisha had direct connection to the chariots of fire. There is an account in Second Kings chapter 6 where Benhadad, the king of Syria, sent his army after Elisha. Elisha's servant was alarmed because the king's army that was sent to arrest them had surrounded the city. Elisha told him not to worry because the ones who were supporting him were more powerful than the king's army. Elisha is obviously referring to the entities in the horses and chariots of fire that had taken Elijah. The servant was not aware of their presence until Elisha requested of Jehovah that he be allowed to see them. Then the servant was able to see what was described as horses and chariots of fire surrounding the area.

I suggest that the horses and chariots of fire were military aircraft using cloaking technology. They were invisible until Elisha's request to Jehovah that they be seen. Elisha further demonstrated his connection with the occupants of the horses and chariots of fire when upon his request they made the king's army go blind and he and his young servant led them astray into Samaria.

Section 4
Elisha Has Two Bears Attack Children That Mocked Him

One of the first things Elisha did as the new prophet of Israel was have two she bears maul forty-two children who were teasing him. The account may be read in Second Kings 2:23–24.

What kind of person would have two bears maul forty-two children for mocking him? This also begs the question, How did Elisha manipulate the two bears into attacking the forty-two children? I reckon that this was done with some type of advanced technology (Goldbaum, 2010).

Section 5
Jehovah Practices Artificial Conception

A reoccurring theme in the Bible is one where a woman is said to be barren until Jehovah decides to make her pregnant. One example is Sarai (also known as Sarah) in Genesis chapters 16, 17, and 21, where it says she was barren until she finally gave birth at the age of ninety years; her husband Abraham (also known as Abram) was one hundred years old. Sarah could not conceive for all those years until she was visited by Jehovah.

Abraham's son Isaac married Rebekah, but she was barren as his mother, Sarah, had been. Nevertheless, God intervened as he had with Sarah, which resulted in Rebekah giving birth to the twins Esau and Jacob. This is described in Genesis 25:21.

Isaac's son Jacob married Rachel, but she was also barren as his mother, Rebekah, and his grandmother Sarah had been. Jehovah again intervened, and Rachel gave birth to Joseph. This is described in Genesis 29:31 and Genesis 30:22-24

In Judges chapter 13, a man named Manoah had a wife who was also barren until Jehovah once again intervened, and she gave birth to Samson.

In First Samuel chapters 1 and 2, Hannah was one of the two wives of Elkanah and was barren until the Lord again intervened, and she gave birth to the prophet Samuel.

Mary, the mother of Jesus in the New Testament, was also made pregnant by Jehovah allegedly without having sexual intercourse. The difference between Mary and the other women mentioned is that she was not said to be barren. She was engaged to Joseph who became upset when he found out she was pregnant while allegedly being a virgin (Matthew 1:18–19).

I suggest that, considering the advanced technology inferred in the Bible, all these women were artificially impregnated.

CHAPTER 9

THE TRUTH ABOUT
JESUS ACCORDING TO
BIBLICAL SCRIPTURE

Section 1
There Is More Than One Son of God in the Bible

The belief that Jesus is Jehovah's only son is the basis of Christianity. I was taught this at an early age as part of my indoctrination into the Roman Catholic Church. I still remember part of the prayer called the Apostles Creed that was used during this indoctrination. It begins like this, "I believe in God the Father Almighty Creator of Heaven and earth; and in Jesus Christ His only Son."

As a matter of fact, Bible scripture says that Jehovah had several sons as written in Genesis 6:2, "That the sons of God saw the daughters of men that they were fair" and in 6:4, "There were giants in the earth in those days; and also after that, when the sons of God came in unto the daughters of men, and they bare children to them."

Sons of Jehovah are also mentioned along with Satan in Job 2:1. The Bible says several times that there was more than one son of Jehovah. It specifically states in the book of Genesis that some of these sons of Jehovah had children with women. It also indicates in the first two chapters in the book of Job that they would meet with their father Jehovah and Satan to discuss matters on earth.

Regardless of the literal evidence, the dogmatic, religious mind will insist on arguing that these sons of God are an entirely different matter than Jesus, the son of God. They will try to convolute the discussion by insisting that Jesus was unique because he was conceived by the Holy Ghost.

My response to this is that we are all unique and we all have a soul. In other words, we all have a Holy Ghost, and it is unique for each one of us. When we physically die, the ghost/soul that occupies our physical body goes wherever it wants or needs to go. That is our true holy ghost. The dogma of the Holy Ghost is just another attempt at mind control by the religious part of the trinity of control discussed in chapter 4, sections 12, 13, and 14 of this book.

Logically speaking, we were all conceived by two holy ghosts, our father and our mother. When they had sex to conceive us, their physical bodies were occupied by their souls; they were not zombies. Any other form of conception is artificial. In my opinion, the natural way is the best way. It is not the only way, but it is the best way. In this regard, I agree with the idea that sex is sacred.

Section 2
According to the Bible, There Is More Than One Jesus Christ

Is there more than one Jesus Christ in the Bible? This is a very important question to most Christians because the idea that Jesus Christ is the only son of the man of war Jehovah is the basis of Christianity. The common belief of most Christians is that there is only one son of Jehovah in the Bible, and his name is Jesus Christ, and he is born and dies only within the New Testament of the Bible.

As a matter of fact, there is another character referred to as Jesus Christ mentioned in Second Esdras 7:28-29. Ecclesiasticus 46:1-8 describes Jesus as the successor of Moses and also his success on the battlefield. Numbers chapter 14 describes an account in which the

Israelites began to rebel against Moses. Joshua and Caleb are mentioned as two characters that helped to put down the rebellion. These same two characters are mentioned in Ecclesiasticus 46:1-10 which includes a reference to the same incident of rebellion. The same character called "Joshua" in Numbers 14:6 is called "Jesus" in Ecclesiasticus 46:1. Jesus and Caleb are again mentioned in First Maccabees 2:55-56 where Jesus is said to have been made a judge in Israel "for fulfilling the word."

Section 3
Jesus Is Joshua, and Joshua Is Jesus

According to the Bible narrative, Joshua the son of Nun or Jesus the son of Nave was a member of the group of Israelites that came out of Egypt. He was part of the exodus during the time of Moses approximately fifteen hundred years before the birth of Jesus of the New Testament. He and Caleb, son of Jephunne, saved Moses from a rebellious mob that was going to kill Moses and return to Egypt (Numbers 14:1–9). After Moses died, Jesus became the leader of Israel and began the killing and plundering of the indigenous peoples of the so-called Promised Land. He was a warmonger who initiated wars on behalf of his alleged father Jehovah, the man of war. Jehovah supported him in his military assaults with hailstones and great stones from heaven in the conquest of Bethhoron and other cities. He was also given an advanced weapon that was used in the killing and plundering of the indigenous Middle Eastern tribes.

Let's compare Joshua, the son of Nun, from the book of Joshua to Jesus, the son of Nave, from the book of Ecclesiasticus:

1. Joshua 10:7–14

   So Joshua ascended from Gilgal, he, and all the people of war with him, and all the mighty men of valour. And the Lord said unto Joshua, Fear them not: for I have delivered them into thine hand; there shall not a man of them stand before thee. Joshua therefore came unto them suddenly, and went up from Gilgal all night. And the Lord discomfited them before Israel, and slew them with a great slaughter at Gibeon, and chased them along the way that goeth up to Bethhoron, and smote them to Azekah, and unto Makkedah. And it came to pass, as they fled from before Israel, and were in the going down to Bethhoron, that the Lord cast down great stones from heaven upon them unto Azekah, and they died . . . Then spake Joshua to the Lord in the day when the Lord delivered up the Amorites before the children of Israel, and he said in the sight of Israel, Sun, stand thou still upon Gibeon; and thou, Moon, in the valley of Ajalon. And the sun stood still, and the moon stayed, until the people had avenged themselves upon their enemies. Is not this written in the book of Jasher? So the sun stood still in the midst of heaven, and hasted not to go down about a whole day. And there was no day like that before or after it, that the Lord hearkened unto the voice of a man: for the Lord fought for Israel.

2. Ecclesiasticus 46:1–8

Jesus the son of Nave was valiant in the wars, and was the successor of Moses in prophecies, who according to his name was made great for the saving of the elect of God, and taking vengeance of the enemies that rose up against them . . . How great glory gat he, when he did lift up his hands, and stretched out his sword against the cities! For the Lord himself brought his enemies unto him. Did not the sun go back by his means? And was not one day as long as two? He called upon the most high Lord, when the enemies pressed upon him on every side; and the great Lord heard him. And with hailstones of mighty power he made the battle to fall violently upon the nations, and in the descent of Bethhoron he destroyed them that resisted . . . In the time of Moses also he did a work of mercy, he and Caleb the son of Jephunne, in that they withstood the congregation, and withheld the people from sin and appeased the wicked murmuring.

Basing on the above Bible narrative, it can be said that Jesus is the same character as Joshua. Yeshua is the Hebrew name for Joshua, and the English spelling of Yeshua is Jesus (Fairchild, 2019). We can deduce from the above verses and other biblical descriptions that this Jesus/Joshua is a man of war as his alleged god and father Jehovah. In both of the above accounts, Jesus/Joshua is leading an army who slaughtered tens of thousands of people while being supported by Jehovah, who provided devastating destruction from the sky with heavy aerial bombardment. Jesus/Joshua was supported by Jehovah with advanced military technology as they massacred tens of thousands of men, women, children, and animals as they plundered the wealth from the cities they destroyed.

It is reasonable to interpret the hailstones and great stones from heaven as a metaphoric description of modern aerial bombardment. Jehovah provided this aerial bombardment that guaranteed Jesus and the Israelites' conquest of the indigenous peoples. Jesus/Joshua was provided superior military assistance just as Moses had been before him and King David among others after him. This same Jesus/Joshua of the Old Testament was mentioned again in First Maccabees 2:55, "Jesus for fulfilling the word was made a judge in Israel." He is mentioned among a list of names as one of the fathers of the Jewish religion that includes Abraham, Joseph, Daniel, and Caleb, who was with Jesus/Joshua in the above accounts.

Jesus/Joshua was mentioned again in the book Second Esdras. The description of this Jesus/Joshua closely resembled the Jesus of the New Testament. Here, according to the story, Jehovah sent an angel to speak to Esdras where he referred to Jesus as his son and Christ. He also mentioned the resurrection and judgment day as written in Second Esdras 7:28–37:

> For my son Jesus shall be revealed with those that be
> with him, and they that remain shall rejoice within four
> hundred years. After these years shall my son Christ die,
> and all men that have life. And the world shall be turned
> into the old silence seven days, like as in the former

judgments; so that no man shall remain. And after seven days the world, that yet awaketh not, shall be raised up, and that shall die that is corrupt. And the earth shall restore those that are asleep in her, and so shall the dust those that dwell in silence, and the secret places shall deliver those souls that were committed unto them. And the most High shall appear upon the seat of judgment, and misery shall pass away, and the long suffering shall have an end . . . Then said I, Abraham prayed first for the Sodomites, and Moses for the fathers that sinned in the wilderness: And Jesus after him for Israel in the time of Achan.

According to the biblical narrative, the Jesus mentioned here is the same aforementioned Joshua/Jesus the prophet in the book of Joshua—the same Jesus who had Achan and his entire family stoned and burned to death as punishment for keeping some gold and silver that they had helped plunder from the inhabitants of Jericho after slaughtering all the men, women, children, and animals (Joshua chapters 6–7). According to the book of Joshua 24:29, Joshua/Jesus died at the age of 110 years old.

In Second Esdras 7:28–30, an angel speaking on behalf of Jehovah said that his son Jesus Christ will be revealed and, after four hundred years, will die along with everybody else and that "the world shall be turned into the old silence for seven days, like as in the former judgments" where no one remains. This sounds like a period of extinction where there is no one left on earth. Note that the narrative is inferring that there have been other similar judgments before the one that is being described. Then in Second Esdras 7:31 to 35, the angel describes that after seven days, there will be a resurrection and judgment. According to the biblical timeline, this prophecy is told approximately 1,000 years after the death of Joshua/Jesus in the book of Joshua 24:29 and approximately 450 years before the birth of Jesus of the New Testament. According to the New Testament, Jesus only lived for 33 years, not over 400 years as stated in the Old Testament Second Esdras 7:28–29. Joshua/Jesus in the book of Joshua lived for 110 years (Joshua 24:29).

According to the Bible narrative, there have been more than one Jesus Christ, and there have been more than one end-of-the-world extinction period, resurrection, and judgment day.

Section 4
The New Testament Jesus Arrives to Continue the Disunity, Chaos, and War That His Father Jehovah Began in the Old Testament

Christianity refers to Jesus as the Prince of Peace. It preaches that Jesus came to the world to teach love and peace. It says that Jesus was basically a pacifist that teaches one to turn the other cheek when slapped. They say that the only time he became violent was when he threw out the money changers, a.k.a. bankers from Herod's temple.

Because Christianity has become the largest and most influential religion in the world, one would think that peace and love would be dominating the global, social, and political landscape. The irony is that since the time of the New Testament Jesus, governments seem to have become more oppressive and violent both in domestic and foreign policy. Modern technology has made governments more efficient in their violence and oppression. In the following scriptures, Jesus said he came to promote war not peace. He came to instigate conflict and create disunity and enemies within the family. He also insisted that everyone needs to love him more than their own family. According to scripture, he was as deranged as his father Jehovah as written in Matthew 10:34–37:

> Think not that I am come to send peace on earth: I came not to send peace, but a sword. For I am come to set a man at variance against his father, and the daughter against her mother, and the daughter-in-law against her mother-in-law. And a man's foes shall be they of his

own household. He that loveth father or mother more
than me is not worthy of me: and he that loveth son or
daughter more than me is not worthy of me.

When we follow the Judeo-Christian storyline of Jehovah and Jesus
from the beginning to the present, Jesus's mission is the continuation,
spread, and perpetuation of what his father Jehovah began in the Old
Testament. The Old Testament is filled with mass murders, infanticide,
genocide, wars, famine, pestilence, lies, deception, slavery, and practically
every crime against humanity imaginable. All these crimes have been
and continue to be perpetuated against humankind around the earth
by the same countries that spread Christianity around the earth. It is
the opposite of what the vast majority of the human population desire,
which is to live in peace, to know truth, to love and be loved, and to
live in freedom and liberty.

Loving your father, mother, daughters, sons, sisters, brothers, wives,
husbands, friends, and people in general is a major reason for human
existence. The arrogance of Jesus to demand that we must love him more
indicates that he is just an extension of his warmongering father Jehovah
of the Old Testament—the arrogant, narcissistic, psychopathic, self-
appointed so-called God of the Jewish, Christian, and Islamic religions.

Jehovah is a god of war, hate, misery, famine, and pestilence. He
may better be described as a demon than a god. This is a man of
war who orchestrates the brutal murders of infants, children, women,
men, and animals and then demands to be worshipped and obeyed
without questioning. This is a god who demands human and animal
blood sacrifice and encourages the plunder of our earth. We have been
bamboozled into accepting and glorifying his psychopathic behavior for
an empty promise of everlasting peace, love, and happiness for everyone
that submits 100 percent to his sadistic commands. The spread of
the Judeo-Christian and Muslim religions has been the spread of war,
famine, and pestilence (disease).

Jehovah of the Old Testament and Jesus of the New Testament
prophesy, war, famine, and pestilence as punishments to people for
not being submissive and obedient enough. As described in the book

of Revelation and other scriptures, this evil demon god will remain in control of human society as long as dogmatic biblical scripture (the script) is followed and acted out by people.

Section 5
A Deceitful Manipulator

I submit the following verses attributed to Jesus as an invitation from a deceitful manipulator luring humans into a mind trap:

> All things are delivered unto me of my Father: and no man knoweth the Son, but the Father; neither knoweth any man the Father, save the Son, and he to whomsoever the Son will reveal him. Come unto me, all ye that labour and are heavy laden, and I will give you rest. Take my yoke upon you, and learn of me; for I am meek and lowly in heart: and ye shall find rest unto your souls. For my yoke is easy, and my burden is light. (Matthew 11:27–30)

Let us paraphrase the above scripture into plain language:

> I exist because of my father Jehovah: and no human really knows what I am about except my father; and no human knows what my father Jehovah is about except me Jesus, and whomever I decide to let know. Join me, everyone that finds life difficult and I will make things better for you. Wear my yoke and be like me; I am overly submissive, spiritless, and with a docile heart: Be like me and you will find rest in your souls. Because my life is easy.

I suggest that the story of the New Testament Jesus is part of the grand deception of a demonic entity that has deceitfully manipulated its way into the consciousness of billions of humans worldwide. It is part of the ongoing process of governmental control of the minds of humanity. This deception to control is described by Carlos Castaneda as the "predators from the cosmos" (Castaneda, 1998) and by Paul Levy as "Wetiko" described as a parasitical psycho-spiritual virus in Native American mythology that feeds on greed and other self-destructive human behavior (Levy, 2017). It is the matrix in the movie *The Matrix*.

Section 6
Jesus Is Not the Only Biblical Character to Raise the Dead

As part of my Christian indoctrination, I was taught that Jesus is the only person to have ever raised the dead. In fact, according to Bible scripture, there is a story in Second Kings 4:32–35 where Elisha the prophet brings a dead child back to life:

> And when Elisha was come into the house, behold,
> the child was dead, and laid upon his bed . . . Then
> he returned, and walked in the house to and fro; and
> went up, and stretched himself upon him: and the child
> sneezed seven times, and the child opened his eyes.

On another occasion, after the same prophet Elisha had been dead and buried for some time, a dead man comes back to life after his body comes into contact with the bones of Elisha. This account may be found in Second Kings 13:21.

Section 7
Jesus Is Not the First Biblical Character to Ascend to Heaven

Another belief I acquired growing up as a Christian is that Jesus is the first and only character in the Bible to ascend to heaven. However, in Genesis 5:24, Enoch was taken into heaven around two thousand years before Jesus of the New Testament, "And Enoch walked with God: and he was not; for God took him." Enoch also described many things that were shown to him in the heavens by different angels. These accounts may be read in the book of Enoch.

The prophet Elijah also ascended into heaven. This account may be found in Second Kings 2:11. The prophet Ezekiel was also taken up into heaven. This account is found in Ezekiel 8:1–3 and 11:1.

Section 8
Christianity Adds Guilt to Fear for Better Mind Control

It is obvious that fear is the main motivator for obedience to Jehovah. After the New Testament crucifixion of Jesus Christ and the creation of Christianity, guilt was mixed with fear to create a more efficient dogma for obedience.

Fear is the main emphasis for the Israelites' obedience to Jehovah in the Old Testament. The Christian dogma that he loves humanity so much that he allows his son Jesus to be tortured and murdered to save us from our sins adds sorrow and guilt to fear for more efficient mind control by the new religion, Judeo-Christianity. Fear, torture, murder, sorrow, and guilt—that is, hell of a way to symbolize and express love and peace.

The Jews are indebted to Jehovah for taking them out of Egypt, and the Christians are indebted to the same entity for allowing the Jews to use his son as a blood sacrifice that becomes the basis for Christianity and the ritualistic Catholic Mass. Essentially, the Catholic Mass symbolizes a sacrificial blood ritual that celebrates the torture and murder of Jesus the son of Jehovah. It symbolizes the drinking of his blood and the eating of his flesh. Every day, over a billion Catholics worldwide celebrate this human blood sacrifice every time the Catholic Mass is performed. The rest of the Christian denominations join the Catholics once a year during the Easter holiday on Good Friday to celebrate the blood ritual of their god being tortured and murdered. All this is justified by the dogmatic belief that "it happened to save us from our sins."

The irony that adds to this madness is to celebrate the resurrection of Jesus with the ritual of a rabbit hiding eggs for children to search for. Eating candy rabbits and eggs is all part of the fun of Easter Sunday to celebrate the resurrection of the Christian god, Jesus. Religious dogma is a strange thing—true madness.

Section 9
Was Jesus Gay?

The following biblical scriptures infer that Jesus may have been gay. In John 13:21–25, Jesus and his disciples were discussing what was about to happen concerning his upcoming crucifixion. He had just informed them that one of them was going to betray him:

> Then the disciples looked one on another, doubting of whom he spake. Now there was leaning on Jesus' bosom one of his disciples, whom Jesus loved. Simon Peter therefore beckoned to him, that he should ask who it should be of whom he spake. He then lying on Jesus' breast saith unto him, Lord, who is it?

In the above narrative, Jesus was hanging out with his disciples, and one of them was leaning and lying on his chest. Jesus told them he was "troubled in spirit" and that one of them was going to betray him. The disciples looked at one another, wondering who the traitor was going to be. Simon Peter then told the disciple who was leaning and lying on Jesus's chest to ask him who the traitor would be. The unnamed disciple, while still lying on Jesus's chest, asked him which of them will betray him.

At the risk of being labeled a homophobic, which I am not, when one sees a man lay on another man's chest, it is reasonable to conclude that they have an unusually intimate relationship.

In John 19:26, we read, "When Jesus therefore saw his mother, and the disciple standing by, whom he loved, he saith unto his mother, Woman, behold thy son!"

In this verse, the narrator is emphasizing that the disciple standing by Jesus's mother is the one that Jesus "loved." It is reasonable to presume that this is the same disciple that regularly lay on Jesus's chest.

John 20:2—"Then she runneth, and cometh to Simon Peter, and to the other disciple, whom Jesus loved, and saith unto them, They have taken away the Lord out of the sepulcher, and we know not where they have laid him."

This account happened after Jesus was crucified. It seemed unusual that the narrator named Peter but referred to the other disciple as the one "whom Jesus loved." It stands to reason that this is the same disciple previously described as regularly lying on Jesus's chest and the "disciple whom Jesus loved."

John 21:7—"Therefore that disciple whom Jesus loved saith unto Peter, It is the Lord."

John 21:20—"Then Peter, turning about, seeth the disciple whom Jesus loved following; which also leaned on his breast at supper, and said Lord, which is he that betrayeth thee?"

None of the scriptures named the disciple who Jesus loved following around, who regularly lay on his chest, and who was repeatedly and specifically referred to as the disciple whom Jesus loved. This unnamed disciple was the only one that scripture specifically singled out as the one whom Jesus loved and the only one that lay on Jesus's chest.

There are those who say it was merely incidental that the unnamed disciple was lying on Jesus's chest. They say that the custom at the time when eating supper was to lay on pillows around a short table, leaning on one's elbow, and John lying on Jesus's chest was merely incidental. How do you incidentally, repeatedly for a prolonged period of time, lay on someone's chest? It seems more likely that it was a common occurrence and part of the relationship between Jesus and this unnamed disciple because it is mentioned three times within verses John 13:23 and 21:20. Also emphasized within the same verses is the description of John as "the disciple whom Jesus loved." This description is mentioned five times within these same verses. There is no other disciple in Bible scripture individually noted as being loved by Jesus.

The narrative of John emphasizes that Jesus loved the disciple who regularly lay on his chest and seems to suggest that the unnamed disciple and Jesus were more intimate with each other than with the other disciples. This type of intimacy between two men is not common among heterosexuals and is not described anywhere else in the Bible. In my opinion, based on the description of the relationship between Jesus and his unnamed disciple, it is not unreasonable to suggest that they may have had a gay (homosexual) relationship.

Section 10
According to Jesus, Praying the Rosary Is Vain and Heathenish

The rosary is a Catholic prayer ritual that includes two prayers (the Our Father and the Hail Mary) being repeated a total of fifty-five times. The irony here is that the following is said by Jesus in Matthew 6:7, "But when ye pray, use not vain repetitions, as the heathen do; for they think that they will be heard for their much speaking."

Section 11
Jesus Says He Is More Important Than Your Home and Family

The following scripture is an example of Jesus's effort to increase Jehovah's control over human minds and wealth through fanatical religious teachings: Matthew 19:29, "And everyone that hath forsaken houses, or brethren, or sisters, or father, or mother, or wife, or children, or lands, for my name's sake, shall receive an hundredfold, and shall inherit everlasting life."

Essentially, what Jesus seems to be saying is if you have abandoned your homes, lands, and families for the benefit of this new religion (Christianity), you will be paid a hundred times their worth and will live forever when you die and go to heaven. In the meantime, we will be making use of all the material wealth you leave us. Recall that the Christian church founders were having their members submit all their wealth to the new church under the penalty of death (Acts 4:32–35 and 5:1–11).

Section 12
Jesus Says You Have to Hate Your Family and Yourself to Be His Disciple

Luke 14:26 says, "If any man come to me, and hate not his father, and mother, and wife, and children, and brethren, and sisters, yea, and his own life also, he cannot be my disciple."

Are you serious? What an absolutely miserable concept! This is another blatant example of Jehovah's demand for total control of the individual and collective minds of humanity. Jesus demanding that you hate yourself and sacrifice the love of your family in order to become the disciple of a murdering psychopath who calls himself God is the epitome of deceptive, narcissistic evil. I suggest it to be a recipe for the creation of mind-contolling cults.

Section 13
According to First Corinthians, Jesus Should Be Ashamed for Having Long Hair

Just about every picture of Jesus that I have ever seen shows him with long hair. The irony of this is found in First Corinthians 11:14, "Doth not even nature itself teach you, that, if a man have long hair, it is a shame unto him?"

How does nature teach us this? I think it is safe to say that man is the only creature in nature that creates tools to cut his hair on a regular basis, hence, what a foolish piece of scripture.

Section 14
Contrary to Popular Belief, Jesus Promotes Usury and the Idea of Taking from the Poor to Give to the Rich

Most Christians are familiar with the story of Jesus of the New Testament throwing the money changers (bankers) out of the temple. Contrary to what most people familiar with the story may believe, Jesus actually encouraged the system of usury. This is evident in Matthew chapter 25 where he was telling a parable where he compared the kingdom of heaven to a rich man who leaves his gold with his servants expecting that they invest it in the banking system and return a profit through usury.

In the parable, a rich man gave each of his three servants a certain amount of gold and then went on a trip to another country. When he returned, two of the three servants had invested in the usury system and doubled the amount of gold they had originally received. However, one of the servants did not invest and only returned the original amount given to him. He was severely reprimanded and punished, while the other two who invested in the usury banking system were handsomely rewarded. What may be more of a surprise to many is that in this same parable, Jesus encouraged the idea of taking from those that have less and giving it to those who have more; as in taking from the poor to give to the rich. The following is how the rich man responds to the servant who did not invest in the banking system and only returns the original one talent (75 lbs.) of gold that was left in his care as written in Matthew 25:26–30:

> Thou wicked and slothful servant, thou knowest that
> I reap where I sowed not, and gather where I have not
> strawed; Thou oughtest therefore to have put my money
> to the exchangers and then at my coming I should have
> received mine own with usury. Take therefore the talent
> from him, and give it unto him which hath ten talents . . .
> And cast ye the unprofitable servant into outer darkness:
> there shall be weeping and the gnashing of teeth.

The servant who was given the least amount of gold and who chose not to invest in the financial banking system was called "wicked and slothful" and severely punished. The two servants who were given the most amount of gold, which they then doubled by investing in the usury system, are given the gold of the servant who did not invest in the usury system. The entire story may be read in Matthew 25:14–30.

What about the story of Jesus kicking the money changers out of the temple?

A money changer is someone that, for a fee, changes one currency for another. It is part of the usury banking system. This was a common practice that took place in the least holy part of Herod's temple called the Court of the Gentiles during the time of the New Testament Jesus. The purchase of animals for sacrifice was also conducted there. The entire temple area was about thirty-five acres, so there was plenty of room for sacrificial animals. The temple was separated into fifteen sections with the Court of the Gentiles being the least holy and largest section (Russell, 2019). This area was not just the largest section of the temple, but it was also the loudest and surrounded the other holier sections within the temple area.

So why did Jesus become upset with the money changers to the point of driving them out of the temple? The most practical reason is because it was the Passover holiday, it was extra crowded and loud. It is likely that the noise became so loud it disturbed the holier inner parts of the temple where Jesus was praying to prepare himself as the human blood sacrifice that would initiate Christianity. The excessive noise centered in the Court of the Gentiles and the money changers irritated him to the point of his driving them out.

Section 15
According to Jesus in the New Testament, He
Returned over Two Thousand Years Ago

The biblical apocalyptic end of the world has been predicted throughout the history of Christianity. Many Christians today say that contemporary world events are signs of the end times when Jesus is supposed to return. They then direct us to the Bible as proof. Matthew chapter 24 is one section of the Bible that many of these predictors of the end seem to enjoy quoting. For example, Matthew 24:6–7 and 24:11: "And ye shall hear of wars and rumours of wars . . . For nation shall rise against nation, and kingdom against kingdom: and there shall be famines, and pestilences, and earthquakes, in divers places."

"And many false prophets shall rise, and shall deceive many."

Many Christian fundamentalists today are pleased with wars, rumors of wars, famine, pestilence, and natural disasters because they perceive them as signs that the second coming of Jesus is on the horizon. Many Christian leaders tell their followers to rejoice because the Second Coming is at hand. The irony here is that many or most of these Christian leaders are from the same country that is the biggest source of providing military armaments and conflicts to the rest of the world (Hartung, 2016). Instead of bringing the behavior of their government into question and directing their congregations to petition their government to end its evil behavior, these Christian leaders tell them to rejoice and to keep supporting warmongering government officials that glorify war. The message is that wars and rumors of war are good because it means that the second coming of Jesus is near.

Note: According to Jesus in the gospel, he returned approximately two thousand years ago! This is according to Jesus in the New Testament gospel!

For example, in Matthew 16:28, Jesus says, "Verily I say unto you, There be some standing here, which shall not taste of death, till they see the Son of man coming in his kingdom."

Jesus was saying that some of those who were physically there listening to him would witness his second coming before their death. That was over two thousand years ago.

I don't think any of those people are physically alive today. I don't think any of them lived to be two hundred years old, let alone two thousand. If they are physically here today, it means they have probably reincarnated in a different body.

In Matthew 24:3, Jesus's disciples asked him, When will he return? Jesus responded by describing events that will happen before he returns. Included in these descriptions are wars, rumors of war, earthquakes, famines, and pestilences. He also gave them a similar timetable as before when he said, "Verily I say unto you, This generation shall not pass till all these things be fulfilled" (Matthew 24:34).

A generation is approximately a span of twenty-five years. Therefore, according to Jesus of the New Testament, he returned approximately two thousand years ago.

Section 16
Israel's Savior Has Also Come and Gone

According to the Old Testament, Jehovah gave Israel a savior approximately 865 years before Jesus (Valkanet, 2010). He is unnamed, but he allegedly freed them from the Syrians as written in Second Kings 13:5, "And the Lord gave Israel a savior, so that they went out from under the hand of the Syrians: and the children of Israel dwelt in their tents, as beforetime."

The Jews were expecting another savior during the time of Jesus who they refer to as the Messiah. They were expecting the Messiah to save them from the Romans, which, of course, did not happen. Today, the Jews, Christians, and Muslims in their religious beliefs continue to expect a savior or redeemer. The Jews are expecting the Messiah; the Christians are expecting Jesus; and the Muslims are expecting the Mahdi, who is said will appear and rule for a few years and restore justice before judgment day and the end of the world. There are various differences of opinion concerning the judgment day expected scenarios within Jewish, Christian, and Muslim religious beliefs (Wikipedia, 2019).

Section 17
According to the New Testament, There Are
Approximately 5.3 Billion Antichrists

Every Christian that I have heard discuss the idea of the Antichrist, referring to him as Satan or the devil, regurgitate the dogmatic idea that he will be a political world leader precluding the second coming of Jesus. However, in First John 2:18 and 2:22 it says that there have been and there are many antichrists: "Little children, it is the last time: and as ye have heard that antichrist shall come, even now are there many antichrists." "Who is a liar but he that denieth that Jesus is the Christ? He is antichrist, that denieth the Father and the Son." According to these passages, every person who does not believe that Jesus Christ is their savior is antichrist.

What is the Christ? The word *Christ* comes from the Greek word *Christos*, which means, "anointed one" or "chosen one." Anointing is part of a religious ceremony that includes pouring, smearing, or rubbing oil on the head of someone. It was done by prophets in the Judeo-Christian Bible when declaring a king. Therefore, anyone who does not believe that Jesus is the chosen king of the world is an antichrist.

If we follow the storyline, it begs the question, who chose this Jesus character to be the king of the world? Obviously, the man of war Jehovah and his collaborators did. Taking into account Jehovah's documented history in the Judeo-Christian Bible, I for one refuse to accept this Jesus Christ character or any other character as my king.

Christianity teaches that Jesus Christ is Jehovah's only son who was given to the world to be used as a blood sacrifice for forgiveness of all the times that his covenants or commandments were not followed as dictated. According to the Christian story, these disobediences are called sins and began with Adam and Eve eating from the tree of knowledge, hence the idea of original sin. Christianity teaches that by the human blood sacrifice of Jesus Christ called the crucifixion, all sins were forgiven, and if you do not believe this, you are an antichrist and will be sent to hell to suffer forever after Jesus Christ returns.

There are approximately 7.6 billion people on earth of which approximately 5.3 billion are non-Christian. Therefore, according to the Bible scripture, there are approximately 5.3 billion antichrists on earth today.

Section 18
Some Followers of Jesus Think He Was the
Reincarnation of a Former Prophet

Reincarnation seemed to be a common belief before and during the time of the New Testament Jesus. In Matthew 16:13–14, Jesus asked his disciples who do the people say he was. Their response was that some say he is the prophet Elijah, some say he is the prophet Jeremias, and some say he is John the Baptist. According to the Bible timeline, Elijah had been dead for approximately nine hundred years; Jeremias, for over six hundred years; and John the Baptist, for less than three years.

It seems that the belief in reincarnation was common, and some believed that Jesus was a reincarnation of a previous prophet.

A reference to visitations from characters who had died many years before is also found in the book of Matthew chapter 17 where Jesus takes his disciples Peter, James, and John up on a mountain where they observe him talking with the prophets Moses and Elijah.

The idea of reincarnation is again inferred by Jesus in Matthew 17:12–13:

> But I say unto you, That Elias (Elijah) is come already, and they knew him not, but have done unto him whatsoever they listed, Likewise shall also the Son of man suffer of them. Then the disciples understood that he spake unto them of John the Baptist.

This scripture infers that Jesus and his disciples understand that John the Baptist was the reincarnation of Elias/Elijah, the prophet of the Old Testament that had died about nine hundred years before.

Section 19
Acting Out the Words of Jesus Can Be
Very Foolish and Very Dangerous

Today, there are some Christians in the US who handle poisonous snakes and drink poison as part of their religious ritual based on certain verses in the Bible attributed to Jesus. Though there have been many injuries and some fatalities, they continue to practice this type of Christianity today (Wikipedia, 2019). This type of Christianity is based on the following scriptures in the New Testament:

Mark 16:18. "They shall take up serpents, and if they drink any deadly thing, it shall not hurt them; they shall lay hands on the sick, and they shall recover."

Luke 10:19. "Behold, I give unto you power to tread on serpents and scorpions, and over all the power of the enemy: and nothing shall by any means hurt you."

One of my many job experiences was as an orderly at a state mental hospital. One of the patients there was a handsome young man in his early twenties. When it came to shower time, the young man would always wait until all the other male patients were finished showering and the shower area cleared of all other patients. I later learned that this was approved as part of his treatment plan.

The young man's parents would come to visit him on a weekly basis. During his parents' visits, they would sit out in the patio on a picnic table. They would always carry a Bible with them and would read from it as they sat and visited with their son. After each visit, the young man was left in a very depressed mood, which I found odd. I later learned of the terrible incident that led to the young man's admittance into the mental institution.

During his final year in high school, the young man had sex with his girlfriend. He was admonished by his parents when they learned about the incident. Apparently, this young man was taught as I was taught concerning sex before marriage—that it was a sin called fornication, which could lead to eternal suffering in hell if one does not repent. Subsequently, the young man was overcome with religious guilt and did the following: he drove out to the desert by himself, built a fire, cut his penis off, and threw it into the fire.

He was apparently following the command from Jesus in the following biblical scripture that I can only describe as hyperbolic madness: "Wherefore if thy hand or thy foot offend thee, cut them off, and cast them from thee: it is better for thee to enter into life halt[29] or maimed, rather than having two hands or two feet to be cast into everlasting fire. And if thine eye offend thee, pluck it out, and cast it from thee: it is better for thee to enter into life with one eye, rather than having two eyes to be cast into hell fire" (Matthew 18:8–9).

Also concerning this particular scripture, on February 6, 2018, a twenty-year-old woman high on crystal meth was heard screaming "I want to see the light" outside a South Carolina Christian church. Church members ran outside and found that she had gouged out her own eyes. The young woman later explained that God had told her to do it as a sacrifice (Michael, 2018).

---

[29] Crippled

CHAPTER 10

THE LEGACY OF JEHOVAH

Section 1
The New Testament Is a Continuation of the Old Testament

Judaism and Christianity are immediately connected in the first verse of the first chapter of the New Testament, which states, "The book of the generation of Jesus Christ, the son of David, the son of Abraham." Chapter 1 then goes on and traces the blood ancestors that connect Abraham to Joseph, the stepfather of Jesus.

In the first page of the New Testament, we see a continuation of the senseless slaughter of innocent children described in Matthew 2:16. King Herod had all the children two years old and under who lived in and around Bethlehem killed. This mass murder of children is similar to when Jehovah murdered all the firstborn of Egypt in the Old Testament book of Exodus. And to emphasize his brutality, he even killed the firstborn of the animals of Egypt.

When one considers all of Jehovah's orchestrations of mass killings throughout the Old Testament, it is natural to presume that he also manipulated King Herod into ordering the massive slaughter of all the newborn babies in his kingdom. One might ask why Jehovah would do this if Jesus was the target of this infanticide. A logical answer would be because he was orchestrating the event that included making sure Jesus was not harmed while, at the same time, enjoying a mass blood sacrifice of thousands of infants.

The New Testament connects and justifies King Herod's murder of the newborns with the Old Testament prophecy of Jeremiah as written in Matthew 2:17 concerning this mass murder of infants, "Then was fulfilled that which was spoken by Jeremiah the prophet." This is just a continuation of the Old Testament Jehovah predicting and orchestrating psychopathic, murderous behavior for the New Testament. Jesus's main message in the New Testament is basically a repetition of Jehovah's main message in the Old Testament. The message is more of a command, and there are three parts to this command: fear, worship, and obedience without questioning.

Section 2
The Bible Promotes Misogyny

The fact that Jesus's biological mother's genealogy is ignored while his stepfather's is emphasized is one of the many examples of the disrespect and inferior status women are given in both the Old and New Testaments of the Judeo-Christian Bible. An almost humorous example of male chauvinism is exhibited in Old Testament Judges 9:53–54, where during an assault on a city tower, a woman wounded King Abimelech and he had his armor-bearer kill him, so it would not be said he was killed by a woman. New Testament biblical scripture teaches that women should always be subservient to the men and should not be heard in religious gatherings because it is shameful if she is. Jehovah's law says that the woman should be obedient to the man. A woman should be seen and not heard, and if she wants to learn anything, she needs to ask her husband at home not in church. A woman can never be a teacher or preacher because it was the woman, not the man, who was deceived in the Garden of Eden. This can be read in First Corinthians 11:3, 14:34–35, and 1 Timothy 2:11–14.

A double standard for punishment is found inNumbers 12:1–16 where Moses's brother and sister were criticizing Moses because he married an Ethiopian woman. Jehovah punished his sister Miriam by giving her leprosy for seven days but did not punish his brother Aaron, who was also the creator of the golden calf and the altar to worship it on when the people rebelled against Moses. Recall that Jehovah was so angry he had decided to wipe out all the Israelites and start over with Moses taking the place of Abraham as the seed for his chosen people. According to the account, it was Moses who talked him out of it.

Section 3
Pedophilia and Ritualistic Child Sacrifice
to Jehovah Continues Today

In a village in South Wales England on June 8, 2018, a thirty-eight-year old Christian woman drowned and burned her four-year-old daughter as a sacrifice to Jehovah. She told police that she had visions of angels that told her the sacrifice of her daughter was required in order to prove her faith and that she was being tested by Jehovah. She was also quoted as saying, "I would never harm my daughter but she was born for Jesus, she was put on this earth for Jesus. She is with the angels now" (Curtis, 2018).

In June 2018, a Muslim man in India cut his four-year-old daughter's throat as a sacrifice to his god, Allah, during the Muslim holy day of Ramadan. He claimed that he was directed by God to carry out the act. During interrogation, the man stated, "It is my sheep and I decided to sacrifice it to God as demanded of me. I have not laid my hands on anyone's child and as such, should not be condemned" (Burns, 2018).

On May 1, 1989, a Jewish woman appeared on the *Oprah Winfrey Show* and claimed that she grew up in a family that had been sacrificing infant babies for generations. The woman was said to suffer from multiple personality disorder, which apparently was a result of the ritualistic abuse she suffered as a child at the hands of her parents and other relatives. During the interview, she claimed that she was forced to participate in satanic rituals where she was raped several times as a child and was forced to sacrifice an infant child.

The woman also claimed that there were members in her family who "bred babies" for use in these rituals. She commented, "A lot of the people were overweight, so you couldn't tell if they were pregnant or not, or they would supposedly go away for a while and then come back."

When asked about the whereabouts of her parents, the woman responded that her mother now lives in the Chicago metropolitan area and is on the human relations commission of the town she lives in. She is considered an upstanding citizen, and no one suspects her involvement in these sacrificial rituals. The woman went on to say that there are many other families and individuals involved in these rituals throughout the United States including police, chiefs of police, doctors, lawyers, and other people that no one would ever suspect.

When asked by Oprah what the purpose of these ritualistic infant blood sacrifices were for, the woman responded, "For power" (Phaser, 2016).

Pedophilia and child sacrifice continue today as part of the legacy of the man of war Judeo-Christian god, Jehovah. The following is an excerpt from a November 2013 news article:

> The child sex abuse crisis in ultra-Orthodox Judaism, like that in the Catholic Church, has produced its share of shocking headlines in recent years. In New York, and in the prominent Orthodox communities of Israel and London, allegations of child molestation and rape have been rampant. The alleged abusers are schoolteachers, rabbis, fathers, uncles—figures of male authority. The victims like those of the Catholic priests, are mostly boys (Ketcham, 2013).

Section 4
When Psychopaths Take Control of Government

Since the creation of the modern hierarchical form of government, where authority to rule is determined by wealth and ancestry, war for monetary gain has been a constant. It doesn't matter what the government is labeled; the fact remains that the wealthiest (ruling elite) in society are always in control of governmental policy whether it be a democracy, republic, monarchy, or socialist form of government.

Recall that the most powerful part of the control system of government is money. Politics is not the system of control, just part of it. Politics offers the illusion that politicians are the ultimate authorities of a country's governmental policies. In reality, the ones that hold ultimate authority are the ones that control the most wealth. This is the reason why the man of war Jehovah demanded that all the wealth collected in the plundering of the indigenous peoples of the Middle East go into his treasury. He knew that using fear as a means of control would eventually run its course and the idea of money via the usury system would work more efficiently as a means of control. Politicians are the window dressing for the real power. They are the puppets on a string (money) and the unseen controllers are the puppeteers behind the curtains.

The idea of money is a more effective system of control because it directly and indirectly affects the physical existence of every individual within human society regardless of who they are. Fear can be generated through the idea of money regardless of your religious or political beliefs. Religion and politics need money to function in our society, but money does not need religion or politics to function.

Money determines the leaders of governments. The more power a political office wields, the more money it costs to be elected to that political office. In 2012, it cost an average of $1,689,580 to win a seat in the US Lower House of Congress, $10,476,451 for the Upper House of Congress, and it cost the presidential winner $1.1 billion to campaign for that office (Murse, 2019).

Wealth is always concentrated at the top of the hierarchical pyramid of control. In order to remain in positions of authority, those in the upper sections of the control pyramid must adapt their behavior to accommodate the demands of the controllers of that control system.

The genocidal wars, famines, and diseases occurring in Yemen and other parts of the world today are manifestations of the aforementioned systems of control, their leaders, and their controllers. The term that comes to mind to describe these leaders and controllers is *homicidal psychopaths*. These psychopaths within governmental positions of power have been a constant throughout documented human history. I suggest that is the reason the United States of America has been at war 93 percent of the time in its 243-year history (WashingtonsBlog, 2015). It is also the reason why it is the biggest arms manufacturer and dealer in the world today. In essence, it is the reflection of its god Jehovah, the man of war. To see modern examples of the manifestations of these psychopaths in positions of power, all one has to do is pay attention to today's world political events and the leaders who are being used in orchestrating them. You will see that they are positioned within the most powerful nations of the world—with the United States, United Kingdom, France, Germany, Russia, China, and Israel (with US and UK assistance) at the top of the list. Recall that the man of war Yahweh/ Jehovah/Allah originated with Israel in the Judeo-Christian biblical narrative.

Imperialist societies throughout written history, including the Bible, have been stuck in the repetitive cycle of war, famine, and disease. The United States empire is the most recent and blatant example of this cycle. Just as the Israelites were led out of Egypt by Jehovah to begin their wars of conquest to accumulate wealth and form the kingdom of Israel, the Puritans were led out of England by Jesus to begin their wars of conquest to accumulate wealth and form the empire of the United States of America. The United States is the modern Israel, and Jesus is the modern Yahweh.

Section 5
The Founding of the United States Parallels the Founding of the Kingdom of Israel

One of the first designs for the great seal of the US was proposed by Benjamin Franklin. The design was described in the following quote by the historian Benson J. Lossing in 1856:

Moses standing on the Shore, and extending his Hand
over the Sea, thereby causing the same to overwhelm
Pharaoh who is sitting in an open Chariot, a Crown on
his Head and a sword in his Hand. Rays from a Pillar
of Fire in the Clouds reaching to Moses, to express that
he acts by Command of the Deity. Motto, Rebellion to
Tyrants is Obedience to God.

This design was obviously pro-Jewish and was comparing the
American Revolution to the Israelite Exodus in the Old Testament.
Benjamin Franklin's design was eventually rejected for Pierre Eugene
Simitiere's design, which can be seen on the back of the one-dollar
bill. However, Jewish symbolism was maintained in a more subtle
Star of David symbol above the eagle's head. This symbol consists
of 13 five-pointed stars arranged as two overlaying triangles forming
the six-pointed Star of David. These thirteen stars forming the Jewish
symbol Star of David simultaneously symbolize the thirteen original US
colonies. Is this just a coincidence?

Is it just a coincidence that the United States and its mother country,
England, are responsible for the creation of the modern state of Israel? Is
it just a coincidence that the United States has supplied and continues to
supply Israel with state-of-the-art weaponry since its creation in 1948?
This dogmatic support of Israel has continued uninterrupted even
after the cowardly 1967 attack by the Israeli military on the technical
research ship USS *Liberty* that killed thirty-four American servicemen.
There is overwhelming evidence that it was a deliberate attack, but
in order to protect Israel, President Johnson and Defense Secretary
Robert McNamara ordered that the inquiry into the attack conclude
the incident was an accident (BBC, 2012).

Since its creation, Israel has maintained military superiority over
all the other Middle Eastern nations, thanks to US grants of billions of
dollars annually mostly in military aide. It seems that the United States
has taken the role of the biblical god Jehovah in providing superior
military technology to the modern state of Israel.

The following are excerpts from an article written by Rabbi Ken Spiro entitled "The Amazing Story of Jewish Influence on the Founding Fathers of American Democracy" (Spiro, 2001):

> The creation of the United States of America represented a unique event in world history—founded as a modern republic, it was rooted in the Bible . . . These Puritans viewed their emigration from England as a virtual re-enactment of the Jewish exodus from Egypt. To them, England was Egypt, the king was Pharaoh, the Atlantic Ocean was the Red Sea, America was the Land of Israel, and the Indians were the ancient Canaanites. They were the new Israelites, entering into a new covenant with God in a new Promised Land . . . Thanksgiving—first celebrated in 1621, a year after the Mayflower landed— was initially conceived as a day parallel to the Jewish Day of Atonement, Yom Kippur; it was to be a day of fasting, introspection and prayer.

Spiro quotes the following from Gabriel Sivan in *The Bible and Civilization* (p. 236):

> No Christian community in history identified more with the People of the Book than did the early settlers of the Massachusetts Bay Colony, who believed their own lives to be a literal reenactment of the Biblical drama of the Hebrew nation . . . these émigré Puritans dramatized their own situation as the righteous remnant of the Church corrupted by the 'Babylonian woe,' and saw themselves as instruments of Divine Providence, a people chosen to build their new commonwealth on the Covenant entered into at Mount Sinai.

Rabbi Spiro further states,

> The earliest legislation of the colonies of New
> England was all determined by Scripture . . . the New
> Haven legislators adopted a legal code – the Code of
> 1655 – which contained some 79 statutes, half of which
> contained Biblical references, virtually all from the
> Hebrew Bible. The Plymouth Colony had a similar law
> code as did the Massachusetts assembly, which, in 1641
> adopted the so-called 'Capital Laws of New England'
> based almost entirely on Mosaic Law.

The Jewish Bible also significantly influenced the founding of various institutions including Harvard, Yale, William & Mary, Rutgers, Princeton, Brown, King's College (today's Columbia University), Johns Hopkins, and Dartmouth University. Many of these institutions also use Jewish words and symbols as part of their official emblem or seal. For example, Yale University's logo contains a pictogram of an opened Jewish bible showing a Hebrew inscription that translates to Urim and Thummim, which are elements of the *hoshen*, the breastplate worn by the High Priest (bing.com/images 2019).

Yale University was named after the wealthy Puritan and benefactor Elihu Yale, a British merchant, slave trader, and president of the East Indies Company. Though Elihu Yale was a Puritan, the name Elihu originates in the Hebrew language and means "he is my God" (Online Etymology Dictionary, 2019). It is also found in the Old Testament book of Job. His surname Yale is of Welsh and Old English origin and means "heights, upland; fertile moor" (Think Baby Names, 2019). Yael originates in the Hebrew language and means "mountain goat; heights, upland; fertile moor (ibid)."

The Hebrew language was so popular among the leaders of the New England colonies that soon after the American Revolution, there were reports that some of them wanted to substitute Hebrew as the official language of the newly formed United States (Fox, 2016).

Harvard, Yale, Columbia, Brown, Princeton, Johns Hopkins, and the University of Pennsylvania all taught courses in Hebrew. In America, Bible study and Hebrew were course requirements in all these colleges, and students had the option of delivering commencement speeches in Hebrew, Latin, or Greek. Much of the population, including a significant number of the Founding Fathers of the US was alumnus of these American universities. For example, Thomas Jefferson attended William & Mary; James Madison, Princeton; and Alexander Hamilton attended King's College, known today as Columbia University (Spiro, 2001).

An interesting fact concerning the Liberty Bell is that it bears the following inscription from the Old Testament Leviticus 25:10: "And Proclaim Freedom Throughout the Land Unto All the Inhabitants Thereof."

The popular idea that the Pilgrims immigrated to America because of religious persecution is a common theme within the American education system. Two important facts not mentioned is that the *Mayflower* was heavily armed and the trip was financed by a joint-stock company called Merchant Adventurers of London, which later splits into the Virginia Company and the Plymouth Company (Wikipedia, 2018). Essentially, the pilgrims were working for a corporation, and their job was to occupy the land and begin generating wealth for corporate investors. Such were the seminal beginnings of what would grow into the United States government—the modern version of the Old Testament Kingdom of Israel.

It is no wonder that all governments of the world today are manipulated through international financial organizations such as multilateral development banks (MDB), Bretton Woods Institutions, regional development banks, and bilateral development banks and agencies (Wikipedia, 2019). This is another indication that the idea of money is more powerful than the idea of religion and politics.

Section 6
The Separation between Religion and the United States Government Is a Lie

We are taught in the United States that there is a distinct separation between religion and the US government. The only reference in the

United States Constitution concerning separation between religion and government is found in the First Amendment, where it states the following: "Congress shall make no law respecting an establishment of religion, or prohibiting the free exercise thereof" (United States Government, 2009).

In other words, government cannot make a law that establishes (begins, institutes, promotes) or prohibits (interferes with, denies) the free exercise of religion. The truth of the matter is the United States government has promoted Judaism and Christianity since its establishment. God is mentioned three times within the US Declaration of Independence—once in the first paragraph and twice in the last paragraph. Based on the historical connection between Christianity, Judaism, and the United States government, it is reasonable to conclude that the biblical man of war Jehovah is the god referred to in the document. Congress does not need to make a law to promote religion because the politicians have been promoting Judaism and Christianity before and since the Constitution was established.

The intimate connection between Christianity, Judaism, and the United States government is demonstrated to the world every four years when an elected president is sworn into office as he puts his hand on the Judeo-Christian Bible and swears to and asks for the help of the god of that holy book by uttering the phrase "so help me, God." The swearing in of congressional members and Supreme Court judges also follow a similar ritual as that of the US president.

All empires have historically been comprised of the systems of religion, money, and politics. This fact has been demonstrated throughout documented human history and is self-evident. Religion has always played a significant role in empire, and the US empire is no exception.

In an article entitled "Bush: God Told Me to Invade Iraq," President George W. Bush claims that "he was told by God to invade Iraq and attack Osama bin Laden's stronghold of Afghanistan as part of a divine mission to bring peace to the Middle East, security for Israel, and a state for the Palestinians" (Cornwell, 2005). This decision has perpetuated wars in the Middle East that have led to millions of deaths and generated huge profits for the military industrial complex, also known as the merchants of death.

In Cornwell's article, President Bush describes how he prayed for strength "to do the Lord's will." When asked if he had asked his father, former President H. W. Bush, for advice, President Bush replied that his earthly father was "the wrong father to appeal to for advice . . . there is a higher father that I appeal to."

The following quote by President Bush from the same article brings to mind Jehovah, the man of war, requiring more and more human blood sacrifice, "Wars are not won without sacrifice, and this war will require more sacrifice."

Of course, these human blood sacrifices to Jehovah (the man of war) do not include the sons and daughters of the politicians nor of their controllers who decide to go to war. They come from the working class referred to in the Bible as sheep and other types of farm animals.

In an *American Free Press* article by Victor Thorn, President George Bush and Secretary of Defense Donald Rumsfeld are reported to have perceived the Iraq War as a "Christian Crusade." The article describes how Secretary of Defense Donald Rumsfeld sent President Bush "top-secret wartime memos" with cover sheets that mixed biblical scripture and battle photos to present the Iraqi invasion as a "holy Christian Crusade." The article says Rumsfeld appeared to be trying to manipulate President Bush into believing that invading Iraq was God's will.

The following proverb from the Bible appeared on an April 2003 report over a photo of a US soldier near a highway sign pointing to Baghdad, "Commit to the LORD, whatever you do, and your plans will succeed (Proverbs 16:3). The next day, US troops reached the Iraqi capital.

The following biblical quote appeared on an April 3, 2003, memo over a photo of a US tank entering Baghdad, "Open the gates that the righteous nation may enter, the nation that keeps that faith" (Isaiah 26:2). Four months later, during a summit in Egypt, the Palestinian foreign minister said Bush told him he was "on a mission from God" and was getting commands directly from the Lord (Thorn, 2009).

According to a May 29, 2008, article by Jason Leopold entitled "US Soldiers Launch Campaign to Convert Iraqis to Christianity," US soldiers in Iraq were trying to convert Muslims to Christianity soon after the 2003 US invasion of Iraq. They were also planning on doing the same in Afghanistan. They distributed Bibles and other fundamentalist Christian literature translated into Arabic to Iraqi Muslims.

It is reported that Chief Warrant Officer Rene Llanos of the US Army's 101st Airborne Division said that the soldiers who are patrolling and walking the streets of Afghanistan are taking along a copy of the Bible and using it to minister to the local residents. Llanos is quoted as saying, "We need to pray for protection for our soldiers as they patrol and pray that God would continue to open doors. The soldiers are being placed in strategic places with a purpose. They're continuing to spread the Word."

It was also reported that US Marines guarding the entrance to the city of Fallujah have been handing out witnessing coins to Sunni Muslims entering the city that read in Arabic on one side, "Where will you spend eternity?" and the biblical scripture "For God so loved the world, that He gave His only begotten Son, that whoever believes in Him shall not perish, but have eternal life—John 3:16" on the other. Sunni Muslims had recently clashed with the US military after an American soldier had used the Muslim holy book, Koran, for target practice.

In a newsletter published in 2004 by the fundamentalist group International Ministerial Fellowship (IMF), Captain Steve Mickel, an army chaplain, claimed that Iraqis were eager to be converted to Christianity and that he personally tried to convert dozens of Iraqis. According to the IMF newsletter, army chaplain Captain Steve Mickel stated, "I am able to give them tracts on how to be saved, printed in Arabic, I wish I had enough Arabic Bibles to give them as well . . . the hunger for the Word of God in Iraq is very great, as I have witnessed first-hand." Mickel attempted to convert Iraqis while delivering leftover food to local residents from his unit's mess hall. He handed out bibles translated into Arabic in the village of Ad Dawr, a predominantly Sunni territory where Saddam Hussein was captured.

In addition to coins and Bibles, there have been reports of the distribution to Iraqi children of Christian comic books published by companies such as Chick Publications. These inflammatory comic books, published in English and Arabic, not only depict Muhammad but show both Muhammad and Muslims burning in hell because they did not accept Jesus as their savior before they died. Chick Publications states on its website that its literature is desperately needed by Muslims (Leopold, 2008).

This behavior by the American military and Christian organizations parallels the behavior of the Old Testament Jehovah and the Israelites after each invasion of the indigenous peoples. They not only brutally murder the men, women, and children and steal their wealth but also downgrade their religion.

In a more recent example of a US government–elected official using his office to promote war and religion is found in a recent *BBC News* report entitled "Pompeo Says God May Have Sent Trump to Save Israel from Iran." In the interview, United States secretary of state Mike Pompeo agreed with the comparison between President Trump and the Jewish hero Queen Esther.

The interview occurred during the Jewish holiday Purim, which celebrates the biblical rescue of the Jewish people by Queen Esther from the Persians (today's Iranians). Pompeo was asked if Trump may have been raised (by God) like Queen Esther to save the Jewish people from the Iranians. His response was "As a Christian, I certainly believe that's possible . . . I am confident that the Lord is at work here" (BBC News, 2019).

In a *Washington Post* article entitled "Sessions Cites Bible Passage Used to Defend Slavery in Defense of Separating Immigrant Families," US attorney general Jeff Sessions uses biblical scripture in Romans 13 to justify his view concerning border policy (Zauzmer & McMillan, 2018).

President Donald Trump has recently been compared to the biblical character known as Persian king Cyrus in the Old Testament in Isaiah 44:28. He is popular among Jews today because they believe he was used by their god, Jehovah, to facilitate the building of the second temple of Jerusalem around 538 BCE when he allowed the Jews to return to Jerusalem.

The most blatant example of a US-elected public official promoting a religion is when President Trump decided to officially recognize Jerusalem as the capital of Israel and having the US embassy moved there. He has also said that the disputed territory of the Golan Heights should be recognized as Israeli territory. Throughout his presidency, Trump has boastfully and unapologetically demonstrated great favoritism toward the state of Israel in his speeches and political actions. It is obvious that the Jewish interpretation of biblical scripture is the primary source for his and his controllers' political decisions. As a gesture of appreciation for his policies favoring Israel, a group of Jews in Israel (Sanhedrin and the Mikdash Educational Center) are minting a coin with his image alongside the image of Persian king Cyrus (Berkowitz, 2018).

Religious fanatics in Israel and America believe that Trump is being used by the man of war Jehovah to facilitate the building of the third temple in Jerusalem, which will fulfill biblical scripture. They are all doing their best to promote the Jewish and Christian beliefs in the coming of the Jewish Messiah and the Christian Jesus at the end of the world.

"TRUMP WILL START THE END OF THE WORLD, CLAIM EVANGELICALS WHO SUPPORT HIM," those are the headlines from a *Newsweek* article dated January 12, 2018. The following is an excerpt from the article:

> Evangelical Christians overwhelmingly support President Donald Trump because they believe he'll cause the world to end. Many have questioned why devout evangelicals support Trump, a man who has bragged about sexual assault, lies perpetually and once admitted he never asks God for forgiveness. Trump's lack of knowledge of the Bible is also well-known. Nevertheless, many evangelical Christians believe that Trump was chosen by God to usher in a new era, a part of history called the end times (Maza, 2018).

Bible prophecy says that before Jesus returns, there will be wars, disease, famine, natural disasters, and the rebuilding of the Jewish temple that was last destroyed around AD 70. The first four items have been happening for many years. The only event that has not yet happened but is required for the end of the world is the rebuilding of the King Solomon's temple. This cannot happen without the state of Israel controlling Jerusalem. That is why President Trump declared that Jerusalem should be the capital of the state of Israel while moving the US embassy there. Trump's actions excite noncritical-thinking religious fanatics such as evangelicals and others who are anxiously looking forward to the end-of-the-world biblical scriptures being fulfilled. To them, Donald Trump is fulfilling his role as one of the main actors in the script/scripture that is said to have been written by the man of war Jehovah.

In another move that excited evangelicals is President Trump encouraging proposals from some state lawmakers that would allow public schools to offer Bible literacy classes. These proposals would "require or encourage public schools to offer elective classes on the Bible, with a focus on its historical significance" (Samuels, 2019).

In another example of elected federal officials promoting a religion is seen in a *USA Today* article entitled "Vice President Mike Pence Quotes Bible in Response to Being Called Christian Supremacist." Pence is quoted as saying, "Any time I'm criticized for my belief in Jesus Christ, I just breathe a prayer of praise. This is a nation of faith, we'll continue to stand for the things that we believe in" (Groppe, 2018).

US government mind control of its citizens through constant propaganda is necessary in maintaining the military industrial complex that President Eisenhower warned against on January 17, 1961, in his farewell address to the nation. I suggest that political religious monetary complex (PRMC) more accurately describes this syndicate. It is becoming more and more obvious that religion has become a big part of the US government's propaganda machine.

CHAPTER 11

THE GOD OF THE BIBLE IS
JUST A MAN OF WAR

Section 1
According to the Biblical Description of
Jehovah, He Is a Warmonger and a Fraud

"The Lord is a man of war: the Lord is his name" (Exodus 15:3). How much clearer can it be said? After reading the biblical narrative that describes the god of the Bible, how can anyone still use words like *peace, love, truth, happiness,* and *just* to describe him? His actions in the scriptures tell us he is the opposite of what the controllers of government would have us believe. Recall that religion is one-third of the trinity of control made of religion, politics, and money, which together constitute modern government the ultimate system of mind control.

Section 2
Jehovah Orchestrates War to Punish and to Reward

Throughout the Old Testament, Jehovah was the orchestrator of wars that cause at least hundreds of thousands of deaths when rewarding the Israelites for following his covenants. The reward process for following these covenants included Jehovah leading them in committing infanticide, genocide, pedophilia, ripping open pregnant women, dashing small children against the stones, and raping their enemies' wives. Then on the other hand, to punish them for breaking these same covenants, he killed them by the thousands by making them commit genocide against one another, eat their own children, inflict them with disease, create adversaries to attack them, dash their children to pieces, rip open their pregnant women, and rape their wives. In essence, both obeying and disobeying Jehovah's covenants result in nearly every crime against humanity imaginable. These crimes are carried out through the process of war, justifying the description "the Lord is a man of war."

Section 3
Judaism, Christianity, and Islam Are
Rooted in Blood and Violence

The religions of Judaism, Christianity, and Islam are directly rooted in the Old Testament beginning with Adam and Eve. All three venerate the prophets Abraham and Moses. Some say Judaism began around 1800 BC when God allegedly made a covenant with Abraham. Some say it began around 1280 BC when God made a covenant with Moses and the Israelites. Finally, some say it began around 1000 BC when the Kingdom of Israel was established during the reigns of Kings Saul, David, and Solomon. All three events are found in the Old Testament books of Genesis, Exodus, and First and Second Kings.

Christianity is said to have officially begun around AD 33 after the crucifixion of Jesus Christ of the New Testament. Islam is said to have officially begun when Muhammad began teaching around AD 613. These dates may vary according to religious points of view or beliefs.

The establishment and spread of these three religions was bloody and violent as seen throughout the Old Testament concerning the Israelites and Judaism. The beginning of Christianity is rooted in the story of a brutal, sadistic, bloody sacrifice of a character called Jesus.

This human blood sacrifice is proudly displayed in the symbol of the cross. The spread of Christianity and Islam have resulted in some of the bloodiest periods in human history, which includes the Crusades and European imperialism.

The Christian European invasions called European Exploration in high school textbooks is the macrocosm of the brutal Israeli invasions of the indigenous peoples of the Middle East described in the Old Testament (McDougal Littell, 2007). The Judeo-Christian European invasions of the indigenous peoples around the globe were just as brutal as the Israeli invasions described in the Old Testament but at a much larger scale.

Christianity is presented as a religion of love and peace; ironically, the bloodiest wars since its establishment have been orchestrated by Christian nations. For example, the primary initiators and participants of World Wars I and II were the Christian nations of England, France, Germany, Russia, and the United States.

Total estimated casualties for World War I were 15–19 million dead and 23 million wounded. Almost half of the dead were civilians and the majority of those died from famine and disease (Wikipedia, 2019). Numbers vary according to the source.

Total estimated deaths for World War II is 70–85 million, including 50–55 million civilians. Most of the civilians killed were more than likely women and children (Dean, 2018).

The killing continued with the Korean War five years after World War II. Total estimated killed in this war was 2,800,000. More than half of those killed, 1,600,000, were civilians. Most of those civilians were also most likely women and children (Wikipedia, 2019).

The killing continued with the Vietnam War. It is estimated that there were 1,353,000 deaths. There are also tens of thousands of birth defects and debilitating diseases caused by the chemical called Agent Orange that was sprayed on the jungle to kill all the trees and plants. Unfortunately, the Vietnamese people living in the jungle were also sprayed with the poison (Lewy, 2018).

Then, of course, we have the Cold War.[30] The total estimated deaths for the Cold War and all its proxy wars including Korea and Vietnam vary from 11–25 million (Wang, 2017).

Today, these same Christian nations are the main players in the so-called War on Terror. So far the estimated deaths are more than 4 million (Carasik, 2015).

The War on Terror may actually have been the beginning of World War III. Just as the stage was set for World Wars I and II by countries forming military and economic alliances, a similar script (scripture) is being followed in setting the stage for World War III. If World War III does increase in magnitude and turns into a thermonuclear war, instead of millions of casualties as in the first two world wars, there will probably be billions of dead and wounded. The insane reality is that there are many Jews, Christians, and Muslims who hope this end of the world script happens so that their religious scriptures are fulfilled.

According to the book of Revelation in the Judeo-Christian Bible, at least one-half of the earth's human population will die during the end-of-the-world events described in Revelation 6:8 and 9:15. The world population today is estimated at 7,716,287,650 and steadily climbing (Worldometers, 2019). If this script (scripture) is carried out today, at least 3,858,144,150 people will die during the end-of-the-world events described in the book of Revelation. It would be the greatest human and animal blood sacrifice for the war god Jehovah ever.

Section 4
The Perpetuation of War Continues Today

The perpetuation of wars by the governments that claim to be followers of Jehovah continues today. These warmongers are led by the most powerful warmonger of them all, the United States. Recall that President George Bush Jr. claimed that he was told by God to invade

---

[30] The state of political hostility that existed between the Soviet bloc governments and the US-led Western governments from 1945 to 1990

Iraq and attack Osama bin Laden in Afghanistan (Cornwell, 2005). Which god is Bush referring to? He is obviously referring to Jehovah of the Judeo-Christian Bible, the man of war. These wars continue today and have resulted in approximately 2 to 4 million deaths of men, women, and children (MintPress, 2015).

Today in the United States, we have a president in Donald Trump who currently authorized a 350-billion-dollar arms sale to Saudi Arabia. Saudi Arabia is a Muslim country currently controlled by a tyrannical regime that kills people for crimes such as adultery, criticizing the government or religion, drug-related offenses, witchcraft, and other nonlethal crimes. Its military is currently mass murdering men, women, and children in Yemen using the weapons of mass destruction they purchased from the US government.

Saudi Arabia is a Muslim government that refers to its god as Allah. Is this the same god as the god of the Jews and Christians? There is overwhelming scriptural evidence in both the Judeo-Christian Bible and the Koran (Muslim holy book) that all three religions worship the same god. They are different branches from the same tree with the same roots. Though they refer to their god by different names, he is the same man of war of the Old Testament. He promotes war, as historically demonstrated in Exodus, the Crusades, and Jihad. Today these three religions are at the core of worldwide military conflicts today.

President Trump has continued the yearly ritual of giving the oppressive Jewish regime in Israel its yearly billions of dollars in military aid, helping them to continue the murder and oppression of the Palestinian people. The Palestinians are the indigenous people who had occupied the land for more than a thousand years before it was savagely taken from them by European Jews assisted by the US and Britain. Since becoming US president in 2016, Trump continues to maintain the status quo of continuous military conflict around the world on behalf of the aforementioned military industrial complex.

From Revelation 6:8, "And I looked, and behold a pale horse: and his name that sat on him was Death, and Hell followed with him."

I suggest that the United States government is the pale horse, and his current rider is Donald Trump, who is being cheered on by war profiteers and religious fanatics calling for more misery, more death, and more hell. Pat Robertson, their most popular leader, former presidential candidate and founder of the Christian Coalition of America, has twice called for the assassination of the Venezuelan president for not cooperating with the demands of US foreign policy. In August 2005, on his television show *The 700 Club*, he suggested that the United States should kill then Venezuelan president Hugo Chávez for not cooperating with US foreign policy demands. Fourteen years later, Robertson again called for the murder of current Venezuelan president Nicolás Maduro, also because he will not cooperate with US demands (YouTube, 2019). The pale-horse metaphor for the US military in the aforementioned scripture is justified when one looks at the historical fact that it has been at war for 93 percent of its existence (WashingtonsBlog, 2015).

Since its creation, the Judeo-Christian United States government has been directly responsible for the murder of millions of men, women, and children around the world. This murderous behavior includes the genocide of Native Americans, the slave trade, American Civil War, war with Mexico, Spanish-American War, and World Wars I and II. The wars continued with the Cold War period that included the Korean and Vietnam Wars and other proxy wars. The wars continue today with the US War on Terror and all its wars instigated in Afghanistan, Iraq, Libya, Syria, Yemen, and other parts of the world. These wars against humanity by the most powerful country in the world should be expected when one looks at the man-of-war god that the leaders of this government worship.

Since its creation, the United States has been following the script of the Old Testament Israelites in its murderous plundering of indigenous peoples. It is no wonder that they share the same god—Jehovah, the man of war. It is also no wonder that a 2013 WIN/Gallup International survey found that people in sixty-five countries overwhelmingly viewed the United States as the greatest threat to world peace (Post Editorial Board, 2014).

The last US president who honestly tried to break the cycle of war was President John F. Kennedy. I presume this is one of the major reasons why the controllers of the US government decided to have him murdered. He would serve as another human blood sacrifice to their war god, Jehovah.

From a religious perspective, the murder of President Kennedy was orchestrated by Jehovah—the same orchestrator of evil in the Bible—because Kennedy had become an obstacle to the aforementioned cycle of war. President Kennedy was murdered by the warmongers of the military institutional complex. He was planning to order a complete American troop withdrawal from Vietnam and ending the Cold War with the Soviet Union. He was going to promote peace by cooperating with the Russians in space exploration and ordering budget cuts for the military and NASA, which would have seriously reduced the future profits of the war profiteers (Prouty, 2009).

After the murder of President John F. Kennedy, this same organization of war profiteers and merchants of death continue to this day spread and orchestrate wars throughout the world. Recall that since its creation, the United States government has been at war for 93 percent of its existence. This—combined with the facts it is viewed by the rest of the world as the biggest threat to world peace and it is the only country to drop nuclear bombs on another country—justifies its role as the pale horse in the book of Revelation. Donald Trump is its rider today. Who will be its rider after the next US presidential election?

Section 5
War of Terror Continues to Be Orchestrated by Jehovah's Followers Today

The following paraphrase summarizes the popular fabricated narrative created by the propaganda machine called the mainstream media concerning today's war on terror involving Judaism, Christianity, and Islam:

The Jewish government of Israel and the Christian governments of the United States, England, France, Germany, and other western European governments are the good guys; the Muslims are the bad guys. The United States government is the righteous leader that is protecting the world from these evil Muslims and other evildoers.

The War on Terror is more accurately the war of terror perpetrated on the world and led by the Jewish government of Israel, the Christian government of the United States, and the Muslim government of Saudi Arabia. These governments are a major part of the world governmental system of control involved in the so-called War on Terror that began after the orchestrated bombing of the World Trade Center. Their main objective is to maintain governmental control of their respective citizens and as much of the world population as they can. They will use any means necessary in maintaining this control, which includes but not limited to lying, murder, imprisonment, and torture. Many of these government leaders may not be aware that their supposedly sovereign states are only a piece of the overall world system of governmental control. Who or what controls this world governmental system of control?

Section 6
Account of US Military Rescuing ISIS Terrorists Today Is like the Account of Jehovah Rescuing Terrorist Leader Maccabeus in the Old Testament

There is an account in the Old Testament about a Jewish guerilla leader named Judas Maccabeus where he and his men were rescued by Jehovah from defeat on the battlefield (Second Maccabees 10:29–31). Today the same Maccabeus would be called a terrorist. The account described how Jehovah swooped in during a battle and saved him from defeat. In the account, Jehovah appeared from heaven and saved the insurgent leader Judas Maccabeus from the army of the Seleucid Empire of Syria. At one point in his struggle against the Syrians, Maccabeus sought help from Rome, which marked the first step in the eventual takeover of Judea by Rome (Knight, 1998).

Fast-forward approximately 2,100 years and we see a similar account in the same Middle East region described in the following June 22, 2019, *Press TV* news article entitled "US Troops 'Saved' Daesh Terrorists, Leaders from Taliban Siege in East Afghanistan." The following excerpts describing the account parallels Jehovah's coming to the rescue of Maccabeus and plucking him from the battlefield about 2,100 years before:

> US troops in Afghanistan have rushed to help members of the Daesh group following a Taliban operation to purge the terrorists from the country's east, according to Taliban militants . . . The US troops saved them from the siege by helicopters . . . the Taliban had been launching an anti-Daesh operation for one week in Kunar and had surrounded the terrorist outfit's important individuals . . . A large number of Daesh terrorists were rescued by choppers while fleeing a battlefield with Taliban last year in the northern province of Jawzjan."

Just as Jehovah orchestrated wars in the Middle East in the Old Testament with his advanced military technology, the US is doing the same today.

Section 7
It's the Same Old Story

In the Old Testament narrative, Jehovah and the Israelites under the guise of a superior god and a superior people motivated by religious prophecy invaded indigenous Middle Eastern nations to take their wealth. Today, we are witnessing a rerun of the same script/scripture. We have the same god and allegedly the same people who are again being provided with superior military technology to facilitate their dominance of that same region.

Just as we have remakes of old movies using different actors to play the same roles of the original actors, today's world political theater is showing the same old tired movie. The script for the old movie can be found in the Old Testament. Today's remake of that movie is about a superior god and a superior people and how they murder and plunder the indigenous peoples of the world. The new superior god is the same as the old superior god, and his name is still Jehovah or Jesus. The new superior people are the same as the old superior people, and their name is still Israel or USA as described in chapter 10 section 5 in this book.

Biblical and contemporary history is full of psychopathic criminal organizations committing crimes against humanity claiming the name of their so-called god and ethnocentric ideologies as justification for their criminal behavior. It is as if human events are being orchestrated by a criminal syndicate. Any criminal syndicate will continue its criminal activities regardless of how many of its lower members or organizations are eliminated. The key to a society ridding itself of crimes being committed against its population by a criminal syndicate is to eliminate the source of that criminal syndicate. I suggest that the source of the crimes committed against humanity throughout history, including the Bible narrative and contemporary history, is none other than people influenced and controlled by Jehovah the man of war and other similar so-called gods and ideologies.

The tools used to influence and control people both rich and poor into criminal destructive behavior are very powerful because they are made from the people, by the people, and of the people. Their existence is dependent on the people. As mentioned before, these tools are the systems of religion, politics, and money. They are combined to form the ultimate system of control called government. Keep in mind that any tool can be used for good or evil.

Throughout recorded history, governments have always led to the scenario described in the book of Revelation concerning the pale horse accompanied by death and hell. It is no different today. We are headed to fulfilling the same script/scripture that has been repeatedly acted out in the past.

To paraphrase a popular quote, "An example of insanity is to repeatedly attempt to fix a reoccurring problem by using the same system in the same way that caused the problem in the first place." Government can work in a positive, constructive way for all peoples only when it is based on love, truth, and freedom. Unfortunately, this type of government does not exist anywhere in the world today. It seems that the only type of government available anywhere in today's world is the artificial government made up of religion, politics, and money.

Natural government is based on love, truth, and freedom. Anything else is unnatural or artificial. Natural government is the antithesis to the control system of religion, politics, and money. It is the only type of government that allows humans to live in peace while achieving their full human potential. I believe this is the type of government John Locke had in mind when he described the idea that everyone is born with three natural rights of life, liberty, and property. He said that the purpose of government is to protect these rights, and if it fails to do so, people have the right and the duty to overthrow it. Thomas Jefferson paraphrases this idea in the second paragraph of the US Declaration of Independence:

> That all Men are created equal, that they are endowed by their Creator with certain unalienable Rights, that among these are Life, Liberty, and the Pursuit of Happiness—That to secure these Rights, Governments are instituted among Men, deriving their just Powers from the Consent of the Governed, that whenever any Form of Government becomes destructive of these Ends, it is the Right of the People to alter or to abolish it, and to institute new Government (United States Government, 2009).

We must remember that the author of these words was a slave master, as were most of the founders of the United States government, including the first president, George Washington. When these words were written, they were not meant for women, nonlandowners, and nonwhites. The founders were all Christians that regarded the Creator to be the god of the Judeo-Christian Bible.

These are the roots of the metaphoric tree called the United States of America government. It should be no wonder that misogyny, poverty, racism, disease, and war have been a constant throughout US history.

The most important lesson I have learned from the Great Spirit through my biological mother and father is how to turn a negative into a positive. This is why I believe the United States of America government can still be a system that can be used as a tool that all peoples can use to live together in peace while reaching their full potential as individuals and as one people. This can become a reality only if it is rooted in love, truth, and freedom. Perhaps the story of Babel was a period in human history where we were living this way until Jehovah and his accomplices destroyed that reality.

EPILOGUE

Jehovah, the god of the Judeo-Christian Bible is the opposite of what people in general and Christians, Jews, and Muslims in particular have been misled to believe. We have been deceived by religious and government authorities throughout history that the god of the Bible is a just and loving entity. We have been bamboozled; we have been hoodwinked.

This deception continues today. In truth, as you have seen, according to the biblical narrative, Jehovah is a murderous psychopath. His actions and the actions of the biblical Israelites are the actions of warmongering, murderous psychopaths. The evidence is in their religious scriptures. All one has to do is read them with a sober, unbiased frame of mind to understand what they are really saying.

Today, the military industrial complex of the United States of America is the modern version of the Old Testament Israel. It is in the process of plundering the weaker nations of the earth as the Israelites plundered the weaker nations of the Middle East. It is no coincidence that the Bible of the Christians includes the Bible of the Jews, hence the Judeo-Christian Bible.

A modern version of the Old Testament script of war, famine, and disease that was acted out by the Old Testament Israelites is today being followed by the American government and its worldwide military industrial complex. This cycle of war, famine, and disease has been a constant among human imperial governments throughout biblical and modern history. The only way this cycle will ever be broken is by refusing to follow the script.

The fact of the matter is that the Judeo-Christian Bible and the God described therein is a compilation of writings written by men. In the course of time, these writings have been manipulated into the psyche of people through religious, political, and financial organizations constituting governments. The sole purpose of these governments is to control the human population. Mind control is the key, hence the governmental system of control.

I have described how religion, politics, and money were combined to form the most efficient system of controlling the human mind ever developed—modern government. In my opinion, the most efficient system of control in the world today is the United States government. The government system of the US today is a culmination of the historical governments of Sumer, Egypt, Greece, Rome, Britain, and Nazi Germany.

Based on biblical scripture, I have described how the god of the Bible behaves as we would expect an evil demon to behave. According to the biblical narrative he is the source of evil. He works together with and as commander of Satan, sons of God, prophets, angels, and evil spirits to orchestrate the miserable events that cause people to suffer. This is all documented in the sections of the Bible that I have presented in this book. This is the so-called God that billions of people around the world today worship every day. The most powerful governments of the world today are tools of this demonic god. They contest for power just as the gods in the Bible contest for power. When we follow the script of which one emerges as the most powerful, we see that the Jewish Christian god is the one. Jehovah emerges as the most powerful god just as the United States of America has emerged as the most powerful government today. The political leaders who have been recently proclaiming their belief in this god of war as part of their political rhetoric are also the leaders of the most warmongering government in the world today, the USA.

After all is said and done, who or what is the true God, creator of all? In my opinion, the answer is pure and simple. We are individually and together the true god creator of all. Nature is a reflection of creation;

we are a reflection of nature, and nature is a reflection of us. We create and we destroy, just as nature does. The key to peaceful coexistence is balance between perceived opposites. It is our individual responsibility to find that balance within ourselves, that equilibrium that brings peace. Creation is ongoing; it never ends. It is now, yesterday, and tomorrow; it is Spirit. A manifestation of Creation is our consciousness and unconsciousness. Both include the present which is us—individually, as groups, and as a whole. We are at the center; we are the balance that decides which way the scale tilts. We are the battle between good and evil, the light and the dark, negative and positive, the yin and the yang. We are the creator and the destroyer.

WORKS CITED

AskHON. *HISTORY ON THE NET-How Many People Died in WW1.* March 24, 2019. https://www.historyonthenet.com/how-many-people-died-in-ww1 (accessed April 2, 2019).

Bahjat, Mudhaffar. "The Embryo Project Encyclopedia- Sources of Human Psychological Differences: The Minnesota Study of Twins Reared Apart..." *embryo.asu.edu.* October 19, 2017. https://embryo.asu.edu/pages/sources-human-psychology-differences-minnesota-study-twins-reared-apart-1990-thomas-j (accessed April 8, 2019).

Barbe, Nigel Ph.D. *Psychology Today.* August 31, 2018. http://www.psychologytoday.com/us/blog/the-human-beast/201509/what-behaviors-do-we-inherit-genes (accessed April 1, 2019).

BBC NEWS. "BBC NEWS." *www.bbc.com.* March 22, 2019. https://www.bbc.com/news/world-us-canada-47670717 (accessed April 17, 2019).

—. "BBC NEWS- Pompeo Says God may have sent Trump to save Israel from Iran." *www.bbc.com.* March 22, 2019. https://www.bbc.com/news/world-us-canada-47670717 (accessed March 27, 2019).

BBC. "WHAT REALLY HAPPENED: BBC Documentary on the USS Liberty: "Dead in the Water"." *whatreallyhappened.com.* November 30, 2012. www.whatreallyhappened.com/WRHARTICLES/ussliberty.html (accessed May 28, 2019).

Bell, Caleb K. "Religion News Service- Poll: Americans love the Bible but don't read it much." *religionnews.com.* April 4, 2013. https://religionnews.com/2013/04/04/

poll-americans-love-the-bible-but-don't-read-it-much/ (accessed April 3, 2019).

Bennett, De Robigne Mortimer. "Marriage of Mary to Joseph the Carpenter!: Discover The Truth." *Discover The Truth.* September 30, 2013. https://discover-the-truth.com/2013/09/30/marriage-of-mary-to-joseph-the-carpenter/ (accessed May 12, 2019).

Berkowitz, Adam Eliyahu. "BREAKING ISRAEL NEWS Latest News Biblical Perspective." *breakingisraelnews.com.* February 15, 2018. https://www.breakingisraelnews.com/102784/sanhedrin-temple-movement-issue-silver-half-shekel-images-trump-cyrus/ (accessed April 3, 2019).

Bible Charts and Maps, PO Box 171053, Austin, TX 78717. *The Amazing Bible Timeline with World History.* March 27, 2019. http://amazingbibletimeline.com/ (accessed April 1, 2019).

Bing.com. "Images." *bing.com.* July 20, 2017. https://www.bing.com/images/search?q=ancient+rome+dining+customs&qpvt=ancient+rome+dining+customs&FORMS=IGRE (accessed May 7, 2019).

bing.com/images. "Images of yale university logo meaning." *bing.com.* June 13, 2019. https://www.bing.com/search?q=yale+university+logo+meaning&FORM=R5FD&ajf=100 (accessed June 13, 2019).

Botterweck, Hohannes D, Helmer Ringgren, and Josef Fabry Heinz. "Dicover The Truth, Bible: Does Numbers 31:8 Sanction Pre-Pubescent Marriages (Child Marriage)?" *discover-the-truth.com.* November 13, 2013. https://discover-the-truth.com/2013/11/14/bible-does-numbers--3118-sanction-pre-pubescent-child-marriage-2/ (accessed May 26, 2019).

Buck, John. "ECONOMIC PERSPECTIVES." *econoperspectives.blogspot.com.* November 10, 2008. econoperspectives.blogspot.com/2008/11/structure-of-federal-reserve-system.html (accessed June 9, 2019).

Burns, Iain. "Daily Mail." *dailymail.co.uk.* June 10, 2018. https://www.dailymail.co.uk/news/article-5827173/Indian-man-kills-four-year-old-daughter-appease-God.html (accessed April 3, 2019).

Butler, Smedley D. *War is a Racket.* Los Angeles: Feral House, 1936.

Carasik, Lauren. "ALJAZEERA AMERICA- Americans have yet to grasp the horrific magnitude of the 'war on terror'." *america.aljazeera.com.* April 10, 2015. america.aljazeera.com/opinions/2015/4/americans-have-yet-to-grasp-the-horrific-magnitude-of-the-war-on-terror. html (accessed April 2, 2019).

Carroll-Silow, Andrew. "THE TIMES OF ISRAEL." *timesofisrael.com.* March 8, 2018. https://www.timesofisrael.com/who-is-king-cyrus-and-why-is-netanyahu-comparing-him-to-trump/ (accessed April 3, 2019).

Castaneda, Carlos. *The Active Side of Infinity.* Klamath Falls: HarperPerenial, 1998.

CHAPTER 2. SCIENCE NO. 2--THE TRAUMATIZATION & TORTURE OF THE VICTIM. February 4, 2019. https://www. bibliotecapleyades.net/sociopolitica/mindcontrol/chapter02.htm (accessed April 1, 2019).

Cohen, Shaye J. D. "Discover The Truth- Bible: Does Numbers 31:8 Sanction Pre-Pubescent Marriages (Child Marriage)?" *Discover The Truth Web site.* November 14, 2013. https://discover-the-truth.com/2013/11/14/bibl-does-numbers-3118-sanction-pre-bubescent-marriages-child-marriages-2/ (accessed May 29, 2019).

Cornwell, Rupert. "INDEPENDENT- Bush: God told me to invade Iraq." *independent.co.uk.* October 7, 2005. https://www. independent.co.uk/news/world/americas/bush-god-told-me-to-invade-iraq-6262644.html (accessed April 3, 2019).

Cummigs, William. "USA TODAY." *usatoday.com.* May 29, 2018. https://www.usatoday.com/story/news/nation-now/2018/05/29/televangelist-wants-new-jet/653202002/ (accessed April 4, 2019).

Cummings, William. "USA TODAY." *usatoday.com.* May 29, 2018. https;//www.usatoday.com/story/news/nation-now/2018/05/29/televangelist-wants-new-jet/653202002/ (accessed April 3, 2019).

Curtis, Joseph. "Daily Mail." *dailymail.co.uk.* December 14, 2018. https://www.dailymail.co.uk/news/article-649089/Mother-38-deliberately-drowned-four-year-old-daughter-bath.html (accessed April 3, 2019).

Dean, Mack. "WORLD WAR 2 CASUALTIES." *worldwar2facts.org.* October 6, 2018. www.worldwar2facts.org/world-war-2-casualties. html (accessed April 2, 2019).

Desk, MintPress News. *Do The Math: Global War On Terror Has Killed 4 Million Muslims Or More.* August 3, 2015. https://www. mintpressnews.com/do-the-math-global-war-on-terror-has-killed-4-million-muslims-or-more/208225/ (accessed July 8, 2019).

Discover The Truth. "Bible: Child Marriage in Ancient Israelite times--Paedophilia?" *Discover The Truth.* September 14, 2013. https://discover-the-truth.com/2013/09/14/bible-child-marriage-in-ancient-israelite-times-paedophilia/ (accessed June 25, 2019).

Dixon, T. "IB PSYCHOLOGY- Minnesota Twin Study of Twins Reared Apart." *themantic-education.com.* February 11, 2019. https://www. themantic-education.com/ibpsych/2019//02/11/key-study-the-minnesota-twin-study-of-twins-reared-apart/ (accessed April 8, 2019).

Elwell, Walter A. "Baker's Evangelical Dictionary of Biblical Theology." *biblestudytools.com.* 1997. https://www.biblestudytools.com/dictionaries/bakers-evangelical-dictionary/concubine.html (accessed May 18, 2019).

Erlich, Reese. *Children of War the Hidden Killer.* 2003. www.warchildren. org/hidden_killer.html (accessed April 1, 2019).

Fairchild, Mary. "ThoughtCo." *thought.co.com.* March 2, 2019. https:// www.thoughtco.com/jesus-aka-yeshua-700649 (accessed April 4, 2019).

Federal Reserve. "FEDERAL RESERVE EDUCATION.ORG." *federalreserveeducation.org.* November 13, 2018. https://www. federalreserveeducation.org/about-the-fed/structure-and-functions (accessed April 5, 2019).

Fox, Tsivya. *How Hebrew Almost Became The Official Language Of America.* July 27, 2016. https://www.breakingisraelnews.com/72700/american-first-language-hebrew/ (accessed July 28, 2019).

Francis, Taylor &. *Science Daily- Cancer and birth defects in Iraq: The nuclear legacy.* January 3, 2019. https://www.sciencedaily.com/releases/2013/05/130521105557.html (accessed April 1, 2019).

Goldbaum, Ellen. *With Magnetic Nanoparticles, Scientists Remotely Control Neurons and Animal Behavior.* July 6, 2010. www.buffalo. edu/news/releases/2010/07/11518.html (accessed July 4, 2019).

Goleman, Daniel. "The New York Times- Major Personality Study Finds That Traits Are Mostly Inherited." *nytimes.com.* December 2, 1986. https://www.nytimes.com/1986/12/02/science/major-personality-study-finds-that-traits-are-mostly-inherited.html (accessed 4 8, 2019).

Groppe, Maureen. "USA TODAY- Vice President Mike Pence quotes Bible in response tobeing called 'Christian supremacist'." *usatoday. com.* August 31, 2018. https://www.usatoday.com/story/news/ politics/2018/08/31/mike-pence-quotes-bible-response-being-called-christian-supremacist/1161092002/ (accessed April 17, 2019).

Hartung, William D. "Salon, "America is the No. 1 arms dealer: Yet why do trends in weapon exports remain in relative obscurity?" *salon. com.* July 31, 2016. https://www.salon.com/2016/07/30/america_ is_no_1_arms_dealer_yet_why_do_trends_in_weapon_exports_ remain_in_relative_obscurity_partner/ (accessed May 26, 2019).

Hauteclocque, Xavier. "Merchants of Death." *en.wikipedia.org.* May 5, 2019. https://en.wikipedia.org/wiki/Merchants_of_death (accessed May 8, 2019).

Highfield, Roger. *DNA survey finds all humans are 99.9pc the same.* February 4, 2019. http://www.telegraph.co.uk/news/worldnews/ horthamerica/usa/1416706/DNA-survey-finds-all-humans-are-99.9pc-the-same.html (accessed April 1, 2019).

Holloway, April. *The Enigma of the Prehistoric Skulls with Bullet-Like Holes.* August 16, 2014. https://www.ancient-origins-. net/unexplained-phenomena/enigma-prehistoric-skulls-bullet-holes-001979 (accessed July 31, 2019).

Itzhaki, Solomon Rabbi. "Bereishit- Genesis- Chapter 25." *Chabad. org.* April 11, 2019. https://www.chabad.org/library/bible_cdo/ aid/8220/showrashi/true (accessed June 24, 2019).

—. "Bible: Child Marriage in Ancient Israelite times-- Paedophilia?: Discover The Truth." *Discover The Truth.* September 14, 2013.

https://discover-the-truth.com/2013/09//14/bible-child-marriage-in-ancient-israelite-times-paedophilia/ (accessed May 12, 2019).

JEWISH VIRTUAL LIBRARY. "JEWISH VIRTUAL LIBRARY-U.S.- Israel Relations: Roots of the U.S.- Israel Relationship." *jewishvirtuallibrary.org.* April 1, 2019. https://www.jewishvirtuallibrary.org/roots-of-the-u-s-israel-relationship (accessed April 3, 2019).

Ketcham, Christopher. "The Child-Rape Assembly Line." *vice.com.* November 12, 2013. whale.to/c/childrape_assembly_line.html (accessed June 29, 2019).

Knight, George Angus Fulton. "Maccabees Priestly Jewish Familly." *ENCYCLOPAEDIA BRITANNICA.* July 20, 1998. https://www.britannica.com/topic/Maccabees (accessed June 24, 2019).

Lagorio, Christine. "CBS NEWS- Televangelist: Take Chavez Out." *cbsnews.com.* August 23, 2005. https://www.cbsnews.com/news/televangelist-take-chavez-out/ (accessed April 9, 2019).

Leonard, Tom. "Daily Mail- Pastors wield venomous snakes." *dailymail.co.uk.* February 2, 2018. https://www.dailymail.co.uk/news/article-5346615/Pastors-wield-venomous-SNAKES-Americas-Bible-Belt.html (accessed April 3, 2019).

Leopold, Jason. "The Public Record- U.S. Soldiers Launch Campaign to Convert Iraqis to Christianity." *Military Religious Freedom Foundation.* May 29, 2008. militaryreligiousfreedom.org/press-relases/soldiers_campaign.html (accessed April 17, 2019).

Levy, Paul. *Dispelling Wetiko: Breaking the Curse of Evil.* August 2017, 2017. https://www.theosophical.org/publications/quest/3472 (accessed April 1, 2019).

Lewy, Guenter. "WIKIPEDIA- Vietnam War Casualties." *en.wikipedia.org.* November 8, 2018. https://en.wikipedia.org/wiki/Vietnam_War_casualties#Total_number_of_deaths (accessed April 2, 2019).

Lombardo, Crystal. *VISIONLAUNCH.* April 3, 2017. visionlaunch.com/many-people-die-malnutrition-year/ (accessed April 1, 2019).

Malik, Muhammad Faroog-i-Azam. *AL-QUARAN.* Houston: The Institute of Islamic Knowledge, 1997.

Maza, Cristina. "Newsweek." *newsweek.com.* January 12, 2018. https://www.newsweek.com/trump-will-bring-about-end-worldevangelicals-end-times-779643 (accessed April 3, 2019).

McDougal Littel. *The Americans.* Evanston: McDougal Littel, 2007.

McDougal Littell. *World History Patterns of Interaction.* Evanston: McDougal Littel, 2007.

Merriam-Webster. "Meriam-Webster." *Meriam-Webster.com.* November 2, 2017. https://www.merriam-webster.com/dictionary/dash (accessed May 20, 2019).

Michael, Tom and Adu, Aletha. "NEW YORK POST." *nypost.com.* March 11, 2018. https://nypost.com/2018/03/11/woman-who-ripped-her-own-eyes-out-thought-it-was-a-sacrifice-to-god/ (accessed April 2, 2019).

MintPress News Desk. *MPN NEWS.* August 3, 2015. https://www.mintpressnews.com/do-the-math-global-war-on-terror-has-killed-4-million-muslims-or-more/208225/ (accessed April 2, 2019).

Murse, Tom. *How Much Did the Obama Campaign Cost?* July 18, 2019. https://www.thoughtco.com/cost-of-the-obama-campaign-3367606 (accessed July 27, 2019).

News, Wiki. "WIKINEWS- Religious broadcaster Pat Robertson calls for assassination of Venezuela's president." *in.wikinews.org.* August 23, 2005. https://en.wikinews.org/wiki/Religious_broadcaster_Pat_Robertson_calls_for_assassination_of_Venezuela%27s_president (accessed April 15, 2019).

Oline Etymology Dictionary. *Elihu.* July 14, 2019. https://www.etymonline.com/word/Elihu (accessed July 28, 2019).

Phaser, The. "The Phaser." *thephaser.com.* December 14, 2016. thephaser.com/2016/12/shocking-jewish-satanic-ritual-child-sacrifice-featured-on-oprah-winfrey/ (accessed April 3, 2019).

Post Editorial Board. *US is the greatest threat to world peace: poll.* January 5, 2014. https://nypost.com/2014/01/05/us-is-the-greatest-threat-to-world-peace-poll/ (accessed July 9, 2019).

PRB 2014 and 2015 World Population Data Sheets. *DISABLED WORLD towards tomorrow.* March 14, 2019. https://www.

disabled-world.com/calculators-charts/life-expectancy-statistics. php (accessed April 1, 2019).

Prestigiacomo, Amanda. *Both Trump And Clinton Went To Jeffrey Epstein's Sex Slave Island.* May 16, 2016. https://www.dailwire. com/news/5749/both-trump-and-clinton-went-jeffrey-epsteins-sex-amanda-prestigiacomo (accessed July 10, 2019).

Prouty, Fletcher L. *JFK The CIA, Vietnam, and the Plot to Assassinate John F. Kennedy.* New York: Skyhorse Publishing, 2009.

Random House. *Random House Webster's College Dictionary.* New York: Random House Inc., 1992.

RSS. "WORLD WAR 2." *worldwar2-database.blogspot.com.* October 9, 2009. worldwar2-database.blogspot.com/2010/10/world-war-ii-casualties.html (accessed April 2, 2019).

Rudin, Ken. *Congressional Sex Scandals in History.* 1998. https://www. washingtonpost.com/wp-srv/politics/special/clinton/congress.htm (accessed July 10, 2019).

Russell, Rusty. "Bible History Online- Herod's Temple Illustration." *bible-history.com.* April 8, 2019. https://www.bible-history.com/ jewishtemple/JEWISHHerods_Temple_Illustration.htm (accessed April 11, 2019).

Said, Sammy. "R The Richest." *therichest.com.* August 12, 2013. https:// www.therichest.com/rich-list/world/the-10-richest-religions-in-the-world/ (accessed April 4, 2019).

Samuels, Brett. "Information Clearinghouse- Trump touts proposed Bible literacy classes in state schools." *information clearing house. info.* January 28, 2019. http://www.informationclearinghouse. info/50987.htm (accessed April 17, 2019).

Service, Quest News. "Original Biblical Jews were a Black African People." *realneo.us.* April 20, 2010. realneo.us/content/original-biblical-jews-were-black-african-people (accessed April 28, 2019).

Sheetz, Michael. "CNBC." *cnbc.com.* July 27, 2017. https://www. cnbc.com/2017/07/27/raytheon-jumps-to-record-high-ceo-credits-trump.html (accessed April 3, 2019).

Smith, Dennis E. *Bible History Daily- A Feast for the Senses...and the Soul.* January 20, 2019. https://www.biblicalarchaeology.org/daily/

ancient-cultures/ancient-israel/a-feast-for-the-senses-and-the-soul/ (accessed April 10, 2019).

Smith, Greg. "So What Faith." *sowhatfaith.com.* November 11, 2010. sowhatfaith.com/2010/11/13/reading-the-whole-bible/ (accessed April 3, 2019).

Spargo, Chris. *Jeffrey Epstein sex trafficking charges involve dozens of underage victims as young as 14 who claim they were paid to perform rape acts on pedophile, who was hiding out in Paris before his arrest.* July 10, 2019. https://www.dailymail.co.uk/news/article-7220951/Jeffrey-Epstein-charged-sex-trafficking-just-days-records-transported-minors.html (accessed July 10, 2019).

Spiro, Ken Rabbi. "aish.com." *aish.com- History Crash Course #55: Jews and the Founding of America.* December 8, 2001. http://www.aish.com/jl/h/cc/48955806.html (accessed April 3, 2019).

Star, Charlie. "kiwireport." *kiwireport.com.* April 25, 2017. www.kiwireport.com/richest-religious-leaders-world/ (accessed April 4, 2019).

The Federal Reserve. "Federal Reserve System Structure." *image. slidesharecdn.com.* July 17, 2017. https://image.slidesharecdn.com/thefedppt-151029182223-lva1-app6892/95/the-federal-reserve-system-4-638.jpg?cb=1445143002 (accessed April 5, 2019).

"The Physical Appearance of Ancient Israel the Hebrews & The Sons of Ham." *angelfire.com.* www.angelfire.com/ill/hebrewisrael/printpages/phys.html (accessed April 28, 2019).

The Walls of Jericho. April 1, 2019. www.israel-a-history-of.com/ (accessed April 1, 2019).

Think Baby Names. *Yael.* 2019. www.thinkbabynames.com/meaning/1/yael (accessed July 28, 2019).

Thorn, Victor. "American Free Press- Secret Memos Reveal Bush Saw Iraq War as "Christian." *americanfreepress.net.* June 1, 2009. www.americanfrepress.net/html/bush_crusade_179.html (accessed April 17, 2019).

United States Government. "The Constitution of the United States." *U.S. Government Printing Office.* Washington, DC, District of Columbia: 111ᵗʰ Congress, 1ˢᵗ Session, July 29, 2009.

Valkanet, Rich. "Bible Timeline." *biblehub.com.* 2010. http://biblehub. com/timeline/ (accessed March 30, 2019).

Vankin, Jonathan. "INQUISITR- Christian Evangelical Leader Pat Robertson Calls for 'Hellfire Missile' Strike on Venezuela's Nicolas Maduro." *inquisitr.com.* April 7, 2019. https://www.inquisitr. com/5381446/christian-pat-robertson-hellfire-missile-venezuela-nicolas-maduro/ (accessed April 15, 2019).

Wang, Brian. "nextBIGFUTURE- Cold War and War on Terror Casualties and De-escalation." *nextbigfuture.com.* September 16, 2017. https://www.nextbigfuture.com/2017/09/cold-war-and-war-on-terror-casualties-and-de-escalation (accessed April 2, 2019).

WashingtonsBlog, Danios. "Information Clearinghous- America Has Been At War 93% of the Time-222 Out of 239 Years- Since 1776." *informationclearinghouse.info.* February 23, 2015. www. informationclearinghouse.info/article41086.htm (accessed April 14, 2019).

Weber, Jeremy. "Christianity Today." *christianitytoday.com.* June 4, 2013. https://www.christianitytoday.com/news/2013/june/surprising-stats-on-who-reads-bible-from-start-to-finish.html (accessed April 3, 2019).

Wenkel, David. *Palestinians, Jebusites, and Evangelicals-Middle East Quarterly-Summer-Vol.14 #3-pp.49-56.* Summer 10, 2007. https:// www.meforum.org/1713palestinians-jebusites-and-evangelicals (accessed July 2, 2019).

Wikileaks. *Wikileaks iraq Video Gunship killing & US Soldier's Confession.* March 1, 2019. https://www.youtube.com/watch?v=kLic1Y3re-A (accessed April 1, 2019).

Wikipedia . *Wall of Jericho.* November 8, 2018. https://en.wikipedia. org/wiki/Wall_of_Jericho (accessed April 1, 2019).

Wikipedia. "Catholic Church sexual abuse cases." *WIKIPEDIA.* November 8, 2018. https://en.wikipedia.org/wikipedia.org/wiki/ Catholic_Church_sexual_abuse_cases (accessed June 29, 2019).

—. "Helicopter Hieroglyphs." *en.wikipedia.org.* January 12, 20019. https://en.wikipedia.org/wiki/Helicopter_hieroglyphs (accessed April 30, 2019).

wikipedia. "International financial institutions." *WIKIPEDIA*. March 2, 2019. https://en.wikipedia.org/wiki/international_financial_ institutions#Other_regional_financial_institutions (accessed June 22, 2019).

—. "Mahdi." *WIKIPEDIA*. June 20, 2019. https://en.wikipedia.org/ wiki/Mahdi (accessed June 21, 2019).

Wikipedia. "Military- World War I casualties." *military.wikia.com*. April 2, 2019. military.wikia.com/wiki/World_War_I_casualties (accessed April 2, 2019).

wikipedia. "Snake handling in religion." *WIKIPEDIA*. June 6, 2019. https://en.wikipedia.org/wiki/Snake_handling_in_religion (accessed June 12, 2019).

Wikipedia. "Talmud." *WIKIPEDIA*. November 8, 2018. http:// en.wikipedia.org/wiki/Talmud (accessed June 25, 2019).

—. "WIKIPEDIA." *en.wikipedia.org*. November 8, 2018. https:// en.wikipedia.org/wiki/Yeshua (accessed April 4, 2019).

—. "WIKIPEDIA- Black people and Morman priesthood." *en.wikipedia. org*. November 8, 2018. https://en.wikipedia.org/wiki/Black_ people_and_Mormonism_priesthood (accessed April 5, 2019).

—. *Wikipedia- Korean War*. March 25, 2019. https://en.wikipedia.org/ wiki/Korean_War#Casualties (accessed April 2, 2019).

—. "WIKIPEDIA- Mayflower." *en.wikipedia.org*. November 8, 2018. https://en.wikipedia.org/wiki/Mayflower (accessed April 3, 2019).

—. *WIKIPEDIA-World War II casualties*. November 8, 2018. https:// en.wikipedia.org/wiki/World_War_casualties (accessed April 2, 2019).

—. "WIKPEDIA- Company of Merchant Adventurers of London." *en.wikipedia.org*. November 8, 2018. https://en.wikipedia.org/wiki/ Company_of_Merchant_Adventurers_of_London (accessed April 3, 2019).

—. "Yeshua." *en.wikipedia.org*. April 29, 2019. https://en.wikipedia. org/wiki/Yeshua (accessed May 6, 2019).

Wilson, Derek. *Out of the Storm: The Life and Legacy of Martin Luther*. London: Hutchinson 978-0-09-180001-7, 2007.

Wood, Bryant. *Answers IN GENESIS.* April 18, 2017. https://answersingenesis.org/archaeology/the-walls-of-jericho/ (accessed April 1, 2019).

Worldometers. *Current World Population.* July 8, 2019. https://www.worldometers.info/world-population/ (accessed July 8, 2019).

WW1 Facts- Information about the First World War. 2012. ww1facts.net/quick-reference/ww1-casualties/ (accessed April 2, 2019).

YouTube. *NBC NEWS: Hillary Clinton covered up pedophile ring.* June 19, 2019. https://www.youtube.com/watch?v=iathwwlfV9c (accessed July 14, 2019).

—. *YouTube- Pat Robertson calls on the U.S. military to take out Venezuelan President Nicolas Maduro.* April 9, 2019. https://www.youtube.com/watch?v=F3_tJDbiu4 (accessed April 10, 2019).

Zauzmer, Julie, and Keith McMillan. "Washington Post- Sessions cites Bible passage used to defend slavery in defense of separating immigrant families." *washingtonpost.com.* June 15, 2018. https://www.washingtonpost.com/news/zcts-of-faith/wp/2018/06/14/jeff-sessions-points-to-the-bible-in-defense-of-separating-immigrant-families/?utm_term=.de2c7bff4cf2 (accessed March 27, 2019).

Printed in the United States
By Bookmasters